The
FORGOTTEN
CHILDREN

THE
FORGOTTEN
CHILDREN

Hungry. Hopeless. Running for their lives.

VERNON BREWER

BOOKS

PUBLISHED BY WORLD HELP, INC. FOREST, VIRGINIA

ISBN 978-0-9788041-0-4

World Help
1148 Corporate Park Drive
Forest, VA 24551
worldhelp.net

World Help exists to fulfill the Great Commission and the Great Commandment through partnering, training, helping and serving, especially in the unreached areas of the world.

In memory
of the thousands of children who have lost
their lives in the 20-year war in Northern
Uganda. They might be nameless and forgotten
by the world, but God knows their names
and their faces, and He holds them
in the palm of His hand.

contents

acknowledgements

I would like to thank everyone who contributed to this book—you are truly making a difference in the lives of the Forgotten Children of Northern Uganda:

To Alex Mitala and George Piwang, our partners in Uganda ... thank you for showing us "the least of these" and allowing us to partner with you to help the Forgotten Children.

To the 10 courageous pastors and their families who shoulder the majority of the responsibility for the children's centers ... you are literally the hands and feet of Christ to these precious children.

To Cody and Doyle Surratt, and my son, Josh, who were the first to catch this vision ... thank you for making sure the children of Uganda will never be truly forgotten.

To my wife, Patty, and to my children, Noel, Nikki, Jenny and Josh ... thank you for the sacrifices you have made to allow me to travel all over the world. I could do nothing without your love, patience and support.

To my parents, Fred and Vivian Brewer ... you have taught me the value of commitment ... the joy of giving ... a love for all people ... and the necessity of perseverance. My greatest goal in life is to transfer those same qualities to my own children.

To Tom Thompson, Skip Taylor, Ben Moomaw, David Day and the entire World Help team, for working tirelessly to help the Forgotten Children.

To Philip Mitchell and Howard Erickson, for documenting my trips to Uganda, and to Ali Rubin, for your hours of research ... without your hard work, I would be without much of the source material that is the heart and soul of this book.

To my editing team, Nancy Horton, Kristen Taylor, Eric Vess and Shelly Roark ... with your dedication, long hours and fanatical attention to quality and detail, I have been able to tell the children's story.

To Dave Damone, Nikki Hogsed, Jon Hart and the entire *Children of the World* team ... thank you for the wonderful way you cast the vision of the Forgotten Children every day.

To my Executive Assistant, Nikki Hart ... you do an incredible job keeping me organized—thank you!

And to God, who, in His grace, spared my life from cancer, and who knows each forgotten child by name ... thank you for giving me the privilege of sharing your love with those in need.

FOREWORD

I live in a country that is a war zone. Armed soldiers, gunfire and unrest are just a part of everyday life in Northern Uganda.

For 20 years, the government of Uganda and the Lord's Resistance Army have waged violent, bloody warfare in the homes and villages of my people.

On some days, the sights, smells and realities of civil strife can be numbing. But a scene that will never cease to break my heart is that of the "night commuters"—thousands of boys and girls who must flee their homes each evening to sleep in the streets and shelters of nearby towns for safety.

The children of Northern Uganda are the greatest and most precious casualties of this conflict. Their suffering is unbelievable—they have been orphaned, attacked and abused, used as sex slaves, driven from their homes, starved and infected with disease. Yet most of the world has no idea of this great injustice that continues to inflict so much pain on innocent children.

In this book, Vernon Brewer, president of World Help, will take you into this war zone. You will meet these young victims and hear their tragic and horrific stories. You will long to put your arms around them and give them comfort. And the good news is that you can!

Not only is Vernon, my brother in Christ, committed to sharing the story of the Forgotten Children, but World Help has also pledged to help them. You will learn about these amazing children and have the opportunity to touch their lives.

My prayer is that once you've heard their story, you will never forget the children of Uganda.

For the children,

Alex Mitala
Pastor and denominational leader in Uganda

1

FRIGHTENED
and FORGOTTEN

"Ever since I heard about

this story, it has kept me

up at night. If we don't

listen and do something

now, we all are going to

have blood on our hands..."

—Oprah Winfrey

I n the dim light of dusk, they appeared out of the African bush.

Covered in dust and grime from miles of travel, the shadowy visitors descended upon the town. I watched some trudge slowly, methodically down the street with vacant eyes staring straight ahead. Others scurried in, casting nervous glances over their shoulders as if being followed. Thousands made the journey into the town, creating a massive, moving line of bodies that extended into the countryside as far as the eye could see. The sight before me was incredible, unbelievable. I wondered if my eyes were playing tricks on me. It all just seemed too unreal.

But these eerie images, silhouetted by the last fading rays of the sun, were not shadows, ghosts or figments of my imagination. They were frightened children who were very much alive … at least for that night.

I stood on the dirt streets of Gulu in Northern Uganda one hot evening and watched as they flooded in. It was a disturbing scene that will remain burned into my heart and mind forever. As I looked into their weary faces and saw hopelessness, despair and very real fear, I ached to hold and comfort each one.

All around me were children of violence, war, hunger, abuse and disease … the casualties of a brutal 20-year civil war. But sadly, most of the world still has no idea of the pain and tragedy these precious little ones must endure every single day of their short lives.

The boys and girls that crossed my path that day are Uganda's Forgotten Children.

I have personally spoken with many of these desperate young people during my visits to Uganda. I've hugged them. I've prayed for them. And as I listened with tears in my eyes to their unimaginable accounts of abduction, rape and torture, I determined then and there that I would tell as many people as I could about them. Somehow, I was going to help.

I want you to know the story of the Forgotten Children. You won't believe what is happening in this dark corner of the world to the most helpless among us! And you will be forever changed by the resiliency and determination of these children.

Many of them have been abducted by the rebel Lord's Resistance Army (LRA), a band of terrorists bent on destroying the very fabric of society in Northern Uganda. I couldn't believe the stories—thousands of children as

> As I looked into their weary faces and saw hopelessness, despair and very real fear, I ached to hold and comfort each one.

young as 7 or 8, captured and forced to do unimaginable acts of terror to "mold" them into little killing machines. Emotionally scarred for life, they have completely lost their childhoods.

What you learn about the LRA and what they are doing to children will turn your stomach. Some reports estimate that more than 30,000 young boys and girls have died in the conflict.[1] In addition to the abductions and violence of the war, almost 1,000 people die every week in Northern Uganda from malaria, HIV/AIDS and starvation as a direct result of the struggle.[2] The danger of attacks by the LRA has displaced 1.7 million people from their homes and forced them to live in the squalor of Internally Displaced Persons (IDP) camps without adequate food, water or health services.[3]

Those suffering in the IDP camps, the ones who have managed to escape their LRA captors, and the thousands more who flee their homes nightly to avoid being abducted—must have a voice.

Is this another Holocaust? I am asking you to find out for yourself. Whatever you do, you *must* learn the truth about the Forgotten Children.

WALKING TO SAFETY

The phenomenon I witnessed on my first encounter with these desperate children—the sight of so many boys and girls inundating the town—was unbelievable to me.

17

But the scene is actually played out every night across the region. It is a tragic reality for the people caught in the violence of Northern Uganda's war zone.

At the height of the rebel attacks, over 40,000 children, some as young as 5 years old, leave their villages to take refuge in the towns of Northern Uganda for the night and make the trek back home the next morning.[4] It is a grueling journey for these little ones who are already weak from malnutrition and dehydration. Many walk as far as eight miles on their desperate commute.

Why do they travel to these towns every night? These boys and girls are fleeing for their very lives! They are looking for a safe place to sleep—on the streets, in bus parks or in the makeshift shelters of the towns.

In the surrounding villages and camps, the children are at tremendous risk for abduction from violent Ugandan rebels who raid homes, murder and mutilate men and women, and kidnap children. More than 25,000 children ages 7 to 17 have been abducted from towns and camps since the war started in 1986[5] ... and more than 10,000 of those abductions occurred in a period of 18 months between 2002 and 2004.[6]

The danger of raids by rebel soldiers increases at night, but the children can find relative protection in the towns, which are patrolled by local police and government soldiers. So the children make their way into these larger towns and cities for whatever protection they can find.

It is hard to imagine that these children are not safe in their own homes!

After hearing the heartbreaking stories of Uganda's Forgotten Children, I was determined to see the situation for myself. Our World Help partner in Uganda, Alex Mitala, is the leader of a denomination of 10,000 churches spread throughout the country. We have been working with his Good Samaritan Children's Home in Kampala for over five years. After telling Alex that we wanted to do something to help the Forgotten Children, several of our World Help staff members and I chartered a plane to Gulu, where this truly unbelievable tragedy is affecting thousands of children every day.

I was not prepared for what I saw in Gulu, even though I had heard about it, read about it and researched it. To actually see it with my own eyes was indescribable. That first day I was there, over 5,000 children slept on the streets. The government officials told me that there are sometimes as many as 14,000 children that seek refuge in Gulu every night.

I met hundreds who had escaped the LRA. All of them continue to have terrifying nightmares … many couldn't even tell me their stories without breaking down. Their bodies literally shook with their sobs!

Others, like 14-year-old Jack, showed little emotion. He sat stoically as he told me the horrors he was forced to endure. Jack was very young when he was brutally

alex mitala:
our partner in uganda

God has used Alex Mitala to connect the resources and compassion of World Help with the vision and passion of local believers in Northern Uganda to help the Forgotten Children. He introduced World Help to local pastors in the region who desperately want to help these young victims, but who just do not have the resources to do so. Here is a look at one of the blessed individuals we are partnering with to give help and hope to Uganda's children:

Alex was born in 1952, one of 11 children. His alcoholic father left the home when Alex was young, leaving his mother to raise the family. At age 15, Alex dropped out of school and two years later he was a wanted drug dealer—selling drugs to children. By age 20, Alex lay dying of malaria in the jungle, where he had taken refuge from the police. Through his fever he heard a voice saying, "Mitala, if you do not get saved, you will surely die." Alex said he heard this message three times a day for three days. But he had no idea what being "saved" meant! When he was miraculously healed, Alex determined to find out how to be "saved." God led him to a small church where he was saved and eternally changed. Within five years, Alex was smuggling gospel literature to the underground church in Uganda. This time he was an outlaw for Christ!

Alex and his wife, Catherine, are currently raising six biological children and 14 orphans. He is also the chief overseer of an entire denomination in Uganda with over 10,000 affiliated churches.

Alex is the link between World Help and the group of pastors and Christians who are carrying out a vision to establish Good Samaritan Children's Centers that will feed, shelter, clothe, care for and provide medical help and counseling for the traumatized children of Northern Uganda.

awakened out of a sound sleep by rebel soldiers storming into his family's small hut. He and his brother were abducted. "At night, we traveled all around Gulu District. At one time we were attacked by the army, so we had to run for our lives. We went to the river and crossed over on a rope.

"My problem was that I was too young to keep up. I was warned to obey the rules. In the time when we were first abducted, I was told not to run. To show they were serious, one of the rebels killed another child while we were [watching]." Jack paused and grew very still. I gently encouraged him to continue, and when he began speaking again, he would not meet my eyes.

"Now that we were trained as child soldiers, we were commanded to kill civilians. I personally killed three people. I am not happy about it," he paused, his distress evident. "One day, the [government forces] attacked our group and we could not run so we were captured by one leader—this is how I escaped from the rebel group."

Jack finally looked me in the eye and said in a voice that suggested he didn't have the right to hope for help, "Today, I long to go for school. I want to study."

Jack's story and his obvious guilt and shame were heartbreaking. And he is not alone … his story is not unique. So many children in Northern Uganda have experienced the horrors of captivity in the Lord's Resistance Army. Boys so young they can barely comprehend the act of murder are made to participate in the bloodiest of executions to "toughen them up." They must help other children beat to death escapees who are caught. They are given guns and forced to shoot their victims at close range so that blood will splatter all over them.

Many are used as little more than pack mules. They carry heavy guns and ammunition mile after mile without adequate food or water. Soldiers take young girls as "wives"—these little girls are raped and beaten. Many become pregnant and are at risk to join the approximately 100,000 children infected with HIV/AIDS in Uganda.[7]

Those who are lucky enough to escape the clutches of the rebels fear being taken again. They live with nightmares and debilitating guilt.

So, in a desperate struggle for survival, members of Uganda's youngest generation make the long walk to towns like Gulu to find safety each night. Called "night commuters," the walkers travel with only the clothes on their backs and maybe a straw mat to sleep on.

As the day gives way to darkness, the group marching towards safety swells in size and the pace quickens. When the very young ones can no longer walk from weariness, older siblings struggle to carry them into the town.

The fortunate children may find a place to rest in courtyards, shelters or churches, but most of them end up sleeping on the streets without even a blanket for warmth.

Can you imagine thousands of children walking into

your city or town every night at dusk? These children have no real place to live, nowhere to sleep, nothing to eat … and they have no one to care for them or protect them.

Gladys Akanyo, 14, has been a night commuter for two years. She makes the hour walk from Kabalopon each evening. "I come here because we fear the rebels," she said. "If they find people, they kill them. I also go to school with my brother and three sisters. We go home after school, but we come back here as it is not safe. And my parents cannot afford to rent in town. I get tired of walking day in, day out. But we are safe as we walk in a group."[8]

Some of these children are too young to even understand the purpose of their regular commute. They are sent away each evening by their parents and assume it is a normal part of life.

After spending a restless night trying to sleep on the hard ground, packed together so closely you can't walk between them, the children then walk the long miles back home in the morning to go to school or to help their splintered families try to get by.

During one visit to Gulu, I met with Bishop Macleord Ochola II, the former leader of the Anglican Church in Northern Uganda who currently serves as Vice-Chairman of the Acholi Religious Leaders Peace Initiative. We discussed the gravity of the situation Ugandans face on a daily basis, as well as Ochola's desire for reconciliation and peace.

In a 2004 report, Ochola stated, "Most people in

> "I come here because we fear the rebels.
> If they find people, they kill them ...
> I get tired of walking day in, day out.
> But we are safe as we walk in a group."
>
> —Gladys Akanyo, age 14

Northern Uganda spend their miserable nights always in the bushes because of insecurity. A climate of fear reigns supreme over the people's lives in these conflict-, disease-, and insecurity-ridden areas."[9]

The Least of These

While night commuting is a specific sign of the desperate situation Northern Ugandans face, it is by no means the only problem afflicting children in the country. I have discovered that the Forgotten Children face overwhelming odds against their survival in virtually every area of life. The children are:

Orphaned. Nearly 2.4 million children under the age of 15 have lost one or both parents to HIV/AIDS.[10] An overwhelming number of boys and girls that I met in

Gulu had lost family members to the rebels, AIDS, malaria, starvation and typhoid. Many of them had no family to protect them and were making the long trek just for survival.

Refugees International cites almost 1,000 deaths a week from harsh living conditions brought on by the war.[11] The overwhelming number of deaths has left Uganda a nation of orphans. And it is the children who are suffering the most.

When the parents of youth located in IDP camps or in the surrounding areas die—either due to the LRA or from diseases like AIDS—the children are often afraid to return to their villages.

Because they do not know what to do or where to go, the traumatized boys and girls live on the streets. Consumed with the basic needs of survival, the orphans have little time, energy or resources for an education. And they are easy prey for the Lord's Resistance Army looking for replacement soldiers, porters and more.

Hungry and Diseased. Starvation is a rampant killer among the young. Orphaned children have a harder time finding food and securing resources from humanitarian assistance groups. Too many needy children are dying from malnutrition and diseases that stem from complications due to lack of food. Fresh water and food are hard to come by in the IDP camps.

Uneducated. Education is a luxury that is out of reach for many children of Uganda. Because so many of the young people live in IDP camps, they miss out on the opportunities that exist in their home villages. Others, who have not fled their districts, are often unable to leave their homes until their nightly commute for fear of abduction or stray bullets.

Essentially, most of these "night commuters" are not able to go to school; even those who are face an uphill battle. They must work on their homework in the dark and make the long trek back home in the morning to attend class.

This volatile situation offers no hope for the future for these Forgotten Children! And the declining educational opportunities threaten to continue the cycle of illiteracy and poor economic conditions for the region. They live without hope.

One girl shared with me that it had been her dream to go to school. But not only was she an orphan trying to take care of herself, she was also taking care of an orphaned baby. She desperately wanted to continue her education, but her responsibility for the child consumed her days. With a resigned shrug, she told me that her opportunity was gone … her only hope for a bright future was in the education of her adopted child.

In Harm's Way. Aside from the beatings and abuse, children who are abducted and forced to become child soldiers are often in very real physical danger. They can be injured or killed by explosions or be shot in confrontations between the LRA and government forces.

Seen as expendable by the rebels, they are given dangerous jobs that often result in injury or death. They handle loaded weapons, clear mine fields, and test out passageways and routes, which can often be fatal.

In one incident a few years ago, 45 children were killed while checking the safety of a passageway for LRA soldiers. Lt. General Jeje Odongo, a member of President Museveni's Cabinet, said, "The rebels used the children to test whether the swollen river was passable. But the children were swept away and drowned."[12]

Psychologically Damaged. The young kidnapped boys and girls are regularly forced to kill other children who try to escape. Human Rights Watch reports that renegade soldiers would smear the killed child's blood on themselves so they "would not fear death" and to discourage other children from trying to escape.[13]

Child soldiers—who are forced to fight—also take on the duties of raiding villages, lighting huts on fire, and shooting uncooperative family members. They are slaves to the older rebels and must endure rape and beatings. The entire existence of these helpless captives depends on whether or not they do what they are told.

The psychological impact of these horrible experiences on innocent children is severe and debilitating. Bishop Ochola sadly stated, "The abducted children, like young plants, are very vulnerable to have their humanity

> "A voice is heard in Ramah, mourning
> and great weeping, Rachel weeping for her
> children, and refusing to be comforted,
> because her children are no more."
>
> —Jeremiah 31:15

manipulated or twisted and eventually destroyed by incredible trauma that they go through. This shall have serious future consequences.

"[These children] will need long term counseling services in order to help them come out of their trauma and successfully reintegrate into civilian life or civil society."[14]

According to a study published in the medical journal, *The Lancet*, in March 2004, when the abducted boys and girls return home, many suffer from post-traumatic stress disorder from witnessing brutal killings or having been raped, beaten, deprived of water and food or forced to kill.[15]

Even those who escape direct contact with the LRA— the children who remain in the IDP camps—live in perpetual fear of abduction, of their parents' murders, or of the sounds of violence from all too close by. The violence that surrounds them has destroyed any semblance of normal life for these children. They have watched family members murdered and friends dragged away.

I believe the humanitarian crisis in Uganda is literally destroying a generation. These hurting children are "the least of these" Christ spoke of in Matthew 25:40. These are Uganda's Forgotten Children …

… **forgotten by their own people.** For the past 20 years, LRA rebel attackers have claimed to be fighting against the government on behalf of the ethnic Acholi people. But the violence and bloodthirsty raids actually target the Acholi, particularly the little ones.

… **forgotten by their government.** The government of Uganda has been "widely lauded" for being one of the first

"Even up till now, the children still live in fear. They don't know what will happen. They cannot yet go back home. When (the soldiers) come, they abduct children … which is their priority."

—Gulu resident

countries to pass a national IDP policy, and has placed almost two million people in Internally Displaced Persons camps to help protect them from attacks by the LRA.[16] But "the social issues that exist elsewhere in Uganda—domestic violence, rape and child abuse, among others—are exacerbated in the camps."[17]

About 80% of the refugees are women and children who are struggling to survive.[18]

... forgotten by the world. The international community has not made this devastating conflict a priority. In August 2004, the U.S. Government enacted the Northern Uganda Crisis Response Act, which calls LRA terrorism a tragedy. The administration placed the LRA on tier two of its Terrorist Exclusion List, which means the LRA is not considered a threat to U.S. interests and, therefore, is not a high priority.[19] In a nation that values children, how can we allow the beautiful faces of these Ugandan children to become forgotten in one of the worst humanitarian disasters the world has ever known!

"The world needs to wake up to the enormity of the crisis in Northern Uganda," said Carol Bellamy, former executive director of UNICEF. "This is one of the most serious humanitarian emergencies in the world."[20]

Oprah Winfrey recently featured a report on the children of Northern Uganda on her television show. She said, "Ever since I heard about this story, it has kept me up at night. If we don't listen and do something now, we all are going to have blood on our hands ... there is a holocaust going on right now in Africa, and everybody who hears it can no longer say, 'Oh, I didn't know that was going on.'"[21]

Jimmy Kolker, former U.S. Ambassador to Uganda, said in an interview with *Christianity Today*, "People need to see what's happening in Northern Uganda. The suffering of these children is unimaginable. Absolutely, it is important for the public to know about this as a step toward bringing it to an end."[22]

As you learn more about these young victims, your life will be changed forever. I hope you won't be able to ignore the horrific travesty that is affecting thousands of children in Northern Uganda.

The director of Uganda's Children of War Rehabilitation Center, Michael Oruni, wants Christians around the world to understand this tragedy and get involved. He said, "Imagine your own child taken away, being raped as your family is killed in front of your eyes. If it were you, what would you feel like? Kids in Uganda—kids just like yours—are taken every night and enslaved, raped, mutilated, murdered.'"[23]

We wouldn't allow this to happen to our children here in America—so how can we turn our backs on the truly forgotten and helpless children in Northern Uganda?

I ask you to consider how you can make sure these

boys and girls do not fade from our minds and into the African bush.

Uganda's little ones are very real. The pain they suffer every day is real. You can help us make sure they will never be forgotten!

2

TO hell
AND BACK

" They told me that if

I didn't kill my brother

now ... they would kill

me. My brother kept

yelling, 'Do it ... you

will live ... do it!'"

—Moses

As I looked at her, I saw a mere child … shaking and sobbing. Her name was Grace, and her unbelievable story burns in my heart. The memory of that little girl's sad eyes and tear-streaked face will stay with me forever.

When I met Grace in the Northern Ugandan town of Gulu, she was only 13 years old. But in her few short years, she had already lived through more pain and terror than many of us endure in our entire lives.

Born in a remote village in Northern Uganda, Grace lived in a small hut with her family and grew up like most of the children in the area. She loved her mother and father so much and they were all very happy … until a dark night that would change her life forever.

One moment Grace, who was 11 years old at the time, lay snug in her bed with the rhythmic noises of the village at night lulling her to sleep. And in the next instant, the crack of gunfire mixed with yelling and screaming jolted her awake and into a living nightmare. Scary, shadowy images violently stormed into her family's hut.

They were members of the dreaded Lord's Resistance Army—hordes of cold-blooded killers. The rebel LRA soldiers killed her father and severely beat Grace's mother. Then they turned their fury onto the child. They dragged the frightened girl out of the hut and hit her over and over again, telling her they would kill her if she did not do as she was told.

The rebels forced her to carry a weapon and ammunition for their army. She was raped and soon became pregnant by one of the soldiers. Grace had a baby when she was only 12 years old … she was just a child herself! Then Grace was forced to watch while soldiers shot her baby.

I couldn't believe what I was hearing! After they killed her baby, Grace tried to escape, but she was captured and once again severely beaten—she suffered more than 100 lashes. Despite the dangerous consequences, Grace fled again and finally got away. When she returned home, she found that her mother had been stabbed by the rebels and had gone insane. Now Grace has no one to care for her … no one to comfort her as she struggles with nightmares and memories … and no one to protect her from being recaptured by the dreaded LRA.

My son, Josh, was videotaping Grace while she was telling her story. I could tell he was taking it all in. When she finished, he walked away emotionally stunned. He couldn't say a word. There were tears in his eyes.

After we prayed with Grace and comforted her, I went over to Josh and put my arms around him. He blurted out, "Dad, can you believe all this? It's so terrible. Can you believe what she has gone through?" He turned away quietly … I knew he would never forget!

Each of the thousands of boys and girls who take flight each night has a story to tell that will break your heart. They

> "See that you do not look down on one of these little ones. For I tell you that their angels in heaven always see the face of my Father in heaven."
>
> —Matthew 18:10

have inherited a world of civil strife and violence where murder, mutilation and fear are everyday facts of life.

One man I spoke to in the town of Gulu said, "Even up till now, the children still live in fear. They don't know what will happen. They cannot yet go back home. When [the soldiers] come, they abduct children … which is their priority."

According to reports, nearly 90 percent of LRA fighters are enslaved children, kidnapped from their families.[24]

The LRA preys on children because they are so easily influenced. Once they are taken by the rebels, these kids experience hell on earth. Children who refuse to submit or cannot keep up with the rest of the rebels are killed on the spot. Complaining, expressing sorrow or guilt and not following commands are all grounds for instant death.

As soon as they are abducted, children are violently forced to kill their own family members ... their brothers, sisters, mothers and fathers. Any child who is caught trying to escape is brought back to the other young soldiers. These "child soldiers" must then brutally kill the "deserter." Anything becomes a weapon ... knives, sticks, clubs, rocks, even bare hands.

A young boy named Moses told me, "One night, the rebel soldiers barged into our hut and began beating everyone and dragged us out into the open." He watched as they clubbed his mother and father over and over again. They took Moses and his brother away. He was terrified because he had heard about other children who were kidnapped, but he was relieved that at least he wasn't alone—his brother was with him. That instant of relief quickly disappeared.

The rebels suddenly stopped by a small stream and turned to the boys. They put a gun to Moses's head.

As soon as they are abducted, children are violently forced to kill their own family members!

"They told me that if I didn't kill my brother now … they would kill me." Moses could hardly make the words come out of his mouth, he was so ashamed and guilt-ridden.

Moses told me he was crying and kept saying that he couldn't do it, but the soldiers were screaming at him and pushing the end of the gun hard into his head. "My brother kept yelling, 'Do it … you will live … do it!'" Moses said.

Before he knew what happened, Moses had pulled the trigger and his brother was lying in the dirt. With tears flowing down his distraught young face, Moses continued, "He wasn't moving and there was blood running from his chest."

The LRA's goal is to put so much shame and guilt on these young boys and girls that they feel they can never go home again. And for the most part … it works. Moses was visibly shaken as he recounted his tragic story. I gently told him that God understood and would forgive him … it wasn't his fault.

Children like Moses and Grace, who manage to escape from this hellish existence, are often traumatized beyond description. One young girl tried to tell me a little about her experience, but broke down in tears. "When you stay in the bush, they call your name, 'You come first … you go and kill that person.' You did a lot of things that your life can be destroyed." She could say nothing more.

41

World Help's Senior Vice President, Tom Thompson, was with us in Gulu and wrote in his journal:

I had only heard about them ... read about them ... even viewed a documentary about them ... Uganda's Forgotten Children. But now, I was witnessing this experience with my own eyes and ears—and I will truly never be able to forget.

I met Gladys. Tears were streaming down her face when she asked me, "What does this mean? Why are they doing this? I don't understand these things." Gladys was raped repeatedly at 14 years of age and then given to one of the rebel soldiers as his wife.

I could barely contain my emotions as she told me her horrific story. She told me how she was forced to kill three of her friends from her village before the soldiers took her away.

I stood with our World Help team on a hill in the middle of a refugee camp that

could not have been more than 10 acres,
where the local village pastor explained
that there were over 3,500 mud huts
housing nearly 17,000 people. He took us
to visit his modest mud hut church, where
hundreds of these refugee boys and
girls were waiting for us to come and
talk with them. I stood there, in that
sweltering mud hut church building,
with my heart breaking, realizing that
these families had nothing but the hope
that someone would come and bring them
help. I tried to encourage them with my
words, but they spoke to me through their
eyes of pain and desperation ... I will
never forget!

As we flew over Uganda that day, I
prayed, "Lord, please touch me, break my
heart, and give me a love and vision for
these people, to see them as You see them."

Tom will never be the same. He will never forget.

When rebel soldiers descend upon villages, they ravage the helpless people there with atrocities that are almost unspeakable.

I recently heard the story of a little girl named Jennifer Anyayo. The rebels raided her village when she was 9 years old and set her family's home on fire. She suffered severe burns on her face, chest and left hand. Tragically, the rebel soldiers shot and killed her father when he tried to get out of the burning hut.[25]

In addition to murdering the innocent, gang-raping men and women, and burning people alive, the rebels cut off lips, ears, hands, feet and breasts. Witnesses have seen soldiers cut open the bellies of pregnant women and rip out their babies. To keep victims from reporting these crimes, they have also been known to cut holes in the lips and padlock them shut.

But the rebels cannot quiet their innocent victims forever.

The Forgotten Children have bravely shared their stories. Imagine their shaking voices. Picture them wiping away flowing tears as they painfully relive what they saw, what they did, and what was done to them. They have been to hell and back.

Christine Ocero, 25, was abducted by rebels after she had gone to the church to pray and was held for 10 years before she escaped. Now she is staying in the Pabbo

Internally Displaced Persons Camp.

"It was difficult. At one point I was shot in the thigh," she said. "Many people were injured. Two people died. I don't know who shot me. Both sides [the LRA and the national army, the Uganda People's Defence Forces (UPDF)] were firing. [The rebels] kept telling us that the government was killing everybody.

"Kony [the leader of the LRA] says that he hears from the spirits. And what he predicts sometimes happens. People believe it comes from the spirits. God knows how many people were dying. Every other day people were being attacked. We knew that if we escaped we would be killed, either by the government or the LRA. But I got to the point where I just wanted to go home.

"I had a small baby, Amoro. When we finally managed to escape, the baby was 4 years old. I gave birth when we were on the move as the [government forces] were

"We knew that if we escaped we would be killed, either by the government or the LRA. But I got to the point where I just wanted to go home."

—Christine Ocero, age 25

chasing us. One woman delivered the baby and the other removed the placenta using a razor blade. She tied the umbilical cord using a thread. The father was a fighter for the LRA. I was given to him as a 'wife' after two weeks. He sometimes beat me, when I didn't listen to his instructions. He was very old.

"Finally I escaped," Christine said. "People were firing and we just made a dash for it. The [government forces] found us and took us to town. I'm happy that I'm free at last. But I have a lot of difficulties. My parents died and I don't have an older brother or sister. I never went to school. I don't have a house. At the moment I'm staying with my uncle. There's nothing I can do. I want to get land so I can start and do a small something for me and for the baby. The home is very risky. I could be killed because I escaped."[26]

Nancy Auma, 13, lives with her grandmother in Laliya Dwol, more than an hour's walk from the center where she sleeps.

"Rebels murdered my parents two years ago. Many people were killed along with my parents. I managed to run away," she said. "We had already escaped, but we went back to the village and found all the dead bodies.

"My grandma is looking after me as best she can, but she can't meet all our needs. I get very tired [walking to the school and the center]. I go straight to school from here in the mornings then back home and then back here. I like school. I hope that I can build a better life for me in the future. I want to be a nurse so I can better help my people."[27]

Thirteen-year-old Esther Aloyo has made the hour-long trek from her home to Gulu for three years.

"I come here because of the war. The rebels attacked my community at Ariyaya Central. So I come here to protect myself from the rebels.

"My parents both died of HIV/AIDS. My father died when I was 9 years old and my mother died a year later. I don't know if I'm HIV positive. I haven't been tested yet.

"I have five brothers and four sisters. One older brother, who's 15, was abducted by the rebels. He has been gone for two years. He was with two other boys who were killed straight away. We heard news that he was the escort of a rebel who is believed to have surrendered, but he is not back yet."

"Rebels murdered my parents two years ago. Many people were killed along with my parents. I managed to run away. We had already escaped, but we went back to the village and found all the dead bodies."

—Nancy Auma, age 13

Esther said that rebels burned to death her guardians—her father's sister and her husband.

"I have new guardians, but they don't have any money. They want to chase me from the home. They want us to go somewhere else. Sometimes they give us food and sometimes they don't. They say, 'Who are you to ask for it?' Sometimes we borrow food from children here.

"I'd like to continue in school, but I don't know if it's going to be possible with my guardians. They say that me and my sister have to get married as soon as possible."

The lack of food and hard work has taken a toll on the child. "Sometimes I feel sick or just generally weak. On Saturdays, we work in the fields from morning until sunset and that's hard. We are growing sweet potatoes and they are not ready. When they are, the guardians will sell most of them."[28]

Maurice Rackara, 11, is a football fanatic and can be seen every night at the center where he finds shelter kicking around a ball made from old bits of cloth and string.

"I'm from Laliya Dwol, which is a village one and a half hours from the night center and I go back there. My mother has rented a place in town, but there's not enough room for me there. I live in the village with some of my brothers and sisters. My father was killed in the war a long time ago. Four of my brothers also come here. We come because of the war—out of fear of being abducted. When I come here to sleep, I feel protected from the rebels.

> "War is very bad. A lot of people are being killed. People are having to run away from home..."
>
> —Maurice Rackara, age 11

"My friend Vincent was abducted. He was taken to the bush but he escaped and came back. He said life there was very hard. They always had to walk very long distances. And they had nothing to eat. They walked long distances without any water. The leaders kept beating and punishing them."

He continued with a decisive nod. "War is very bad. A lot of people are being killed. People are having to run away from home and squeeze into small houses in town. Whatever you leave behind is always looted.

"I'm in the fourth year at school. I started very late. When my father died my family couldn't afford to send me to school. Not all my older brothers and sisters went to school because there wasn't enough money. I go back to Laliya Dwol most days. Me and my brothers and sisters go back there to farm and then we come back here. I eat once a day with mom. We normally have either grains, beans, vegetables or posho (maize). I've had malaria about five times. I had to go to hospital to get treated."[29]

Can you imagine how greatly God's heart is moved by the suffering of the boys and girls in Uganda? Jesus said, "Let the little children come to me, and do not hinder them, for the kingdom of heaven belongs to such as these" (Matthew 19:14).

What could cause such upheaval and dysfunction in a nation that would leave children like Grace, Moses and others at the mercy of brutal warfare? I soon discovered how a civil uprising has turned into an all-out assault *on* children ... *by* children.

3

TERROR
unleashed

The LRA is one of

the larger terrorist

organizations in the

world and has killed

more people than many

other violent groups.

—*Christianity
Today*

To truly understand the plight of the Forgotten Children, you need to know more about the violent civil war that controls their lives. All the elements involved—a ruthless and mysterious rebel leader, a cult-like and militant army, a defenseless people living in extreme poverty, and a reluctant government—make for a deadly combination. From what I have learned about the 20-year struggle—and seen with my own eyes—the result has been fatal.

So, who is fighting? Why are they fighting? And what is being done about it?

The Lord's Resistance Army (LRA) is a rebel group led by Joseph Kony operating out of Northern Uganda. They are fighting the government's Ugandan People's Defence Forces (UPDF).

Kony practices a spiritual cocktail of Christianity, Islam and witchcraft, and claims that the Holy Spirit directs his military initiatives. He has stated that he wants to overthrow the current government to establish one based on the Ten Commandments. Kony actually claims to be fighting on behalf of the local Acholi people, the predominant ethnic group in the north. But in reality, it is the innocent people who are his main targets for violence and brutality.[30]

Kony's army has inflicted more terror and suffering on the Acholi people than on the government he claims to be

fighting. Today, the nearly one and a half million impover-
ished Acholi people cling to existence in some of the most
deplorable conditions known in human history.

The making of a war

The beginnings of the civil war that rages in Uganda
date back to 1986, when the current president, Yoweri
Museveni, defeated the former rebel leader from the north.
Museveni took power with his National Resistance Army.

The people of Northern Uganda feared a government
they believed to be dominated by western and southern
nationals.

Uganda at a glance

- Uganda is a landlocked country with a
  population of more than 28 million.
- 80% of the population depends on
  agriculture, with coffee as the biggest
  export.
- In 2005, the estimated GDP per capita
  was $1,800.

Source: The World Factbook

The first insurgent group to organize itself in response
was the Uganda People's Democratic Army (UPDA), which

took hold of the northern regions of the country. It was essentially remnants of the ousted troops overthrown by Museveni. This group was soon overshadowed by Alice Auma Lakwena's organization, the Holy Spirit Movement (HSM), and eventually collapsed.[31]

The HSM was very popular with the people of Northern Uganda at first, claiming inspiration from the Holy Spirit. Alice Lakwena declared that she had been given spiritual powers by the spirit "Lakwena" (which means "messenger" in Acholi). Her goals were to cleanse the Acholi of their sins and to fight the oppressive government. The movement posed a considerable threat to Museveni's power in the northern strongholds, but Lakwena was eventually defeated and fled into exile.[32]

That is when her cousin, Joseph Kony, entered the political scene.

Kony: a mysterious evil

Kony was born in the village of Odek in Gulu District. In 1987, at age 26, he took over the remnants of the semi-religious HSM and reorganized the UPDA with fervor and brutality to form the Lord's Resistance Army. Claiming to be a spirit medium, Kony is said to quote the Bible, recite the Rosary, bow toward Mecca like a Muslim, practice witchcraft and fast during Ramadan.[33]

Very few people outside of his circle of trusted

commanders—or his victims—have ever met or even seen Kony. The elusive leader is known to be a practicing polygamist with about 50 captives he claims are his "wives."[34]

He reportedly goes into "trances" for guidance, speaking into a tape recorder and playing back the recordings as military commands. According to one report, Kony also sets fire to toy military vehicles and figurines, predicting the course of battles from the burn patterns.[35] He is also said to use reptiles in magic rituals to detect traitors and make his enemies sick. Kony even claims that he can turn stones into hand grenades![36]

Kony tells his young, cult-like army to cover their skin with oil or "holy water" so that when they go into battle the spirits will protect them. If they are worthy and without sin, the bullets are supposed to bounce off of them. If a soldier is killed, Kony reasons that the person must have had a secret sin in his or her life and deserved to die. He warns children that if they run away, the "baptismal fluids" are always visible to him and that he will be able to find them again.[37]

Kony has surrounded himself with a religious mystique that strikes fear both in his followers and in the Acholi people. His spiritual rituals and brutality give him a psychological hold on the entire region.

One of Kony's trusted bodyguards who eventually escaped, Patrick Komakech, said, "[He was] unique, sometimes normal, possessed by evil spirits, sometimes

KONY'S FIRST MEDIA INTERVIEW IN 20 YEARS

The elusive leader of the LRA, Joseph Kony, gave an unexpected interview to journalist Sam Farmar in June 2006. The two met deep in the jungle of Congo, surrounded by armed rebel soldiers. Following are some excerpts of Kony's quotes from that interview:

"I'm a freedom fighter who is fighting for freedom in Uganda. I am not a terrorist."

Kony claimed he has a negotiating team waiting in Juba, capital of southern Sudan. "Peace talks are good for me. If Museveni [Uganda's president] can agree to talk with me, it is only a very good thing, which I know will bring peace to the people of Uganda."

"I am a human being like you. I have eyes, a brain and wear clothes, but they are saying 'we don't talk with people, we eat people. We are killer.' That is not true. Why do you meet me if I am a killer? ... It's just propaganda. Museveni went into the villages and cut off the ears of the people, telling the people that it was the work of the LRA. I cannot cut the ear of my brother, I cannot kill the eye of my brother. Our wealth, our property, was destroyed by Museveni. He want to destroy all Acholi so that the land of Acholi will be his land. I did not kill the civilian of Uganda. I kill the soldier of Museveni."

Kony's answer to the children who have been abducted by the LRA: "I don't have acres of maize, of onion, of cabbages. I don't have food. If I abducted children like that, here in the bush, what do they eat?"

"We want the people of Uganda to be free. We are fighting for democracy. We want our leader to be elected—but not a movement like the one of Museveni. ... Yes, we are fighting for Ten Commandments. Is it bad? It is not against human rights. And that commandment was not given by Joseph. It was not given by LRA. No, that commandment was given by God."

Kony on spirits: "They speak to me. They load through me. They will tell us what is going to happen. They say 'you, Mr. Joseph, tell your people that the enemy is planning to come and attack.' They will come like dreaming, they will tell us everything. You know, we are guerrilla. We are rebel. We don't have medicine. But with the help of spirit they will tell to us, 'you Mr. Joseph go and take this thing and that thing'."

"Through this peace talk I know that we are going to solve all those things, we are going to solve all those problems." [38]

crazy. He claims his army will overthrow the Ugandan government and replace it with rule by the Ten Commandments. He would use the Bible, but at the same time he was killing people."[39]

The warlord's objectives for the rebel resistance are as vague and bizarre as his personal beliefs. He has no clear "political agenda," but rather speaks in ambiguous, spiritual dimensions. Although he claims to be fighting for Acholi independence, he has declared no political platform or demands upon which to base negotiations for peace. This makes peace dialogue difficult and sustains the devastating conflict.

FROM PEACE TALKS TO MILITARY ACTION

The Ugandan government tried to negotiate with Kony's army by using Betty Oyella Bigombe, a government minister who was responsible for dealing with the insurgency at the time it began.

In November of 1993, Bigombe's representatives and members of the LRA met in the Gulu District of Uganda. Kony's troops asked for amnesty for their men and insisted that they would return home only under the condition that they didn't have to surrender. Bigombe, however, was reluctant to trust Kony and the LRA because she found out he was negotiating with the Sudanese government for assistance and aid in overthrowing Museveni. To add to this suspicion, Kony asked for six months to supposedly gather his men.[40]

Four months later, the LRA ended the negotiations, and Museveni announced a seven-day deadline for the LRA to surrender or face military consequences. The LRA scarcely acknowledged the ultimatum by Museveni and continued their rampage.

Also in 1994, the Sudanese government began supporting the LRA's actions with military assistance and arms and made the strife a regional dispute. Their actions reportedly stemmed from the Ugandan support for the insurgent group, Sudan People's Liberation Army (SPLA), fighting a civil war in the south of their own country.

Crossing the border and setting up camps in Sudan as a safe haven, the LRA built up its membership to an estimated 3,000 to 4,000 members.[41] But the Acholi people soon became weary of the war, lost faith in Kony as their liberator and stopped volunteering. That's when Kony and his commanders began abducting children to fill their depleting ranks and turning on the Acholi with murderous raids.

In 1999, the Ugandan Government attempted to end the conflict in any way possible—and so save the children— by passing an Amnesty Act which protects any LRA fighter who surrenders to the government from prosecution.[42]

In an effort to normalize relations between the two countries, the Sudanese government allowed Uganda into southern Sudan in 2002 to attack the LRA at its bases. Called "Operation Iron Fist," the deployment of as many as 10,000 Ugandan troops into southern Sudan did destroy some of the LRA camps, but it did not destroy the rebel army. Within months, Kony and his militants had increased the violence and frequency of their attacks on the people of Uganda.[43]

In 2004, the Sudan allowed another round of military operations by Ugandan troops within its southern borders.[44] But again, the LRA is still wreaking havoc on the innocent.

In addition to military tactics, there have been numerous attempts by various groups to initiate negotiations between the government of Uganda and the LRA in the past 20 years. In fact, Betty Bigombe, who is no longer a government minister, has met with LRA leaders several more times, at great personal risk, to negotiate a settlement to end the fighting. But neither side has wholeheartedly committed to finding a completely peaceful solution to date.

In late 2005, peace communications completely broke down after the International Criminal Court issued arrest warrants for Kony and his top four commanders.[45]

From my experiences on the ground and what I've been told by government officials, peace does not seem to be a high priority for the rebels. In recent years, Kony has convinced himself that the Acholi people he says he's fighting for are collaborating with the government. So he has unleashed his fury on them. "Alienated from the Acholi, the LRA wages terror on the civilian population as a means to maintain attention and challenge the government."[46]

The brutal and frequent attacks supposedly halt any communication between the civilians and the government by forcing the people to flee their homes. Then, once they are gone, the army loots the village for food and goods they can use or sell.

Kony is killing the Acholi people to prove that the government cannot protect them. He actually believes this will cause citizens to be disillusioned with the government and support his cause instead.

I cannot comprehend this twisted logic. He is murdering people to get their support! Kony and his henchmen are nothing more than cold-blooded murderers. According to *Christianity Today*, the LRA is one of the larger terrorist organizations in the world and has killed more people than many other violent groups.[47]

Despite the LRA's grotesque atrocities, the Acholi people do not support mass military destruction of the rebel forces. Why? Because the army is made up of their own abducted and indoctrinated children … and any such action would be murdering their own family members. The situation has become an unbearable ethical dilemma. The vast majority of rebels are both enemies *and* victims.

In a recent article in *Vanity Fair* titled "Childhood's

End," Christopher Hitchens summarized the dilemma the Acholi people face:

> The Acholi people of Northern Uganda, who are the chief sufferers in all this, have to suffer everything twice. Their children are murdered or abducted and enslaved and then come back to murder and abduct and enslave even more children. Yet if the Ugandan Army were allowed to use extreme measures to destroy the LRA, the victims would be ... Acholi children again. It must be nightmarish to know that any feral-child terrorist who is shot could be one of your own. 'I and the public know,' wrote W.H. Auden in perhaps his greatest poem, 'September 1, 1939':
>
> > What all school children learn,
> > Those to whom evil is done
> > Do evil in return.[48]

LIFe in The LRa

It is hard to wrap my mind around the fact that this brutal killing machine, the LRA, is made up of mostly young people. The heartbreaking fact is that Kony and his militant leaders are training a generation of children to be hardened killers. The vast majority of LRA soldiers—and now even a majority of the rebel commanders—were once abducted children, "brainwashed, brutalized and forced to kill viciously."[49]

As soon as a new group of children are captured, adult commanders force them to carry supplies on a trek through the African bush. They march all day in the heat—without food or water—for up to a week. Their hunger and thirst is so great that the little ones eat leaves to survive or try to find moisture in muddy ditches. The forced march from sunup to sundown causes their bare feet to bleed and swell. But they dare not fall behind. Any child who does or tries to escape is murdered.[50]

The children are beaten regularly to harden them for warfare. They work 12 hours a day at the whims of the rebel leaders.

Children may be murdered for crying or failing to obey commands quickly enough. And what's worse is that it is the other children who must execute them. Under threat of their own death, these babies hack others to pieces with machetes or burn them alive.

One of the "initiations" for captives is that they must kill

"We were beaten all the time, sometimes with clubs, sometimes with pangas. I had to beat another girl until she died—the soldier said he would kill me if I did not make her die. I had to walk for a very long time, carrying heavy things. Once, I was too slow, so they beat me and said they would kill me. I saw them kill others for being too slow."

—Mary, interview with
Christianity Today[51]

another child. Frequently, commanders make children kill their own siblings to erase any family bonds that might interfere with their commitment to the LRA. Afterward, the traumatized children are told that their families and society will never accept them again. It is an effort to give these poor victims so much guilt that they will be resigned to their life in the ranks. It is only the beginning of the nightmare.

LRA child soldiers are forced to attack villages and commit heinous acts—shooting and cutting people, sometimes force-feeding the severed body parts to victims' families.

Others are burned alive or beaten to death with machetes and clubs—the terrorized child soldiers are taught to mutilate the victims beyond recognition.

NOT THE ONLY PROBLEM

For 20 years, the people of Northern Uganda have suffered at the hands of unrestrained violence and oppression. And what makes the situation even more heartbreaking is that these war-weary people must also deal with a host of other conflicts and handicaps to basic survival. Even if the fighting were to end today, and the abductions cease, the North would continue to be ravaged by the consequences of 20 years of upheaval: the destruction of their agrarian-based economy; the lack of opportunities for education; the dissolution of family structures; increasing rates of infection for AIDS and other diseases caused by unsanitary living conditions and lack of medicines; and the persisting psychological trauma of years of abduction and fighting.

Ugandans are besieged by problems that go far beyond the dangers of the war—they need our help.

4

why hasn't
someone done
something?

" The thing to remember

is that there are two

Ugandas ... one of relative

peace, and the one where

children suffer more than

in any country on Earth."

—Rev. Carlos Rodriguez,
executive secretary of
the Justice and Peace
Commission

frica's Friendliest Country! That was the banner headline across the Tourism Uganda website homepage that I called up on the Internet. There were articles and personal testimonials that lauded the praises of Uganda. The promotional photos revealed breathtaking views and action adventures.

I must admit that after seeing the very real suffering of the people of Uganda with my own eyes, I was a little surprised to find images of such an enticing destination pop up on the computer screen before me. I knew I wouldn't find photos of hungry, homeless orphans or bloody battles prominently displayed on the marketing site that was used to attract visitors to the wonderful tourism resources of Uganda. But it sure isn't the same place I have experienced on my many visits to the war-ravaged districts of Gulu, Kitgum, Pader and Lira in Northern Uganda.

Uganda is really a country divided with two different personalities—one of peace and growing prosperity, and another that is torn apart by violence, poverty and upheaval.

The country boasts a lush and serene capital, and the international tourism campaigns lure visitors with slogans such as "Uganda, Gifted by Nature." But in Northern Uganda, most residents survive on food aid and live in congested camps. Government troops patrol the desolate countryside where there is almost no evidence of the agrarian villages that were once home to the camp inhabitants.

"The thing to remember is that there are two Ugandas," the Reverend Carlos Rodriguez, executive secretary of the Justice and Peace Commission, said, "one of relative peace, and then one where children suffer more than in any country on Earth."[52]

Southern Uganda and Western Uganda are the tourist destinations. Northern Uganda is a war zone.

THE BIG QUESTION

One of the questions I get asked frequently is, "Why hasn't anyone done anything to stop all this? Why can't someone end the conflict and suffering?" This is a very difficult question to answer. There are so many historical, cultural, ethnic, political and religious issues at play.

I wish that it were as simple as saying, "The Ugandan army should just go on the offensive and wipe out the LRA," or, "Let's just negotiate a peace settlement," or, "It's time to disband the IDP camps and send the people back to their villages." But unfortunately, none of these one-dimensional solutions will work. As World Vision put it in their publication *Pawns of Politics*, "The misunderstanding has resulted in a tendency to simplify the conflict to merely 'getting the bad guy,' while ignoring the complexities that continue to fuel the conflict."[53]

Many of the perpetrators of the violence were once

innocent children themselves, brainwashed and forced to kill, creating a horrible quandary for all those who want to see the LRA stopped. As one parent in Gulu said, "The children are our children, whether LRA or UPDF. Whose mother do you want to cry? The military solution is no solution for our young people."[54]

The situation is just too complex for easy solutions.

Internally Displaced Persons (IDP) Camps

In a desperate attempt to provide better protection to the people of the North, the government instituted the IDP camps and moved people into them. There are almost 200 camps now, some with populations of just a few hundred, some with thousands of people, and the largest, Pabbo, is home to as many as 63,000.

The IDP camps are composed of mud huts, 10 feet in diameter, with thatched roofs that burn down often. As many as 15 family members are crammed into a single hut.

I have visited many of these camps in Northern Uganda on numerous occasions. The living conditions are horrible and unsanitary ... I have never seen anything else like it in my life. Hundreds of children roam the dirty spaces between huts. Some are clothed in rags; others have no clothes. Many of them are starving; most have coughs or runny noses that indicate they are sick. Others are dying from AIDS and other diseases.

Some have plastic coverings provided by NGO's (nongovernmental organizations), but all provide very little shelter. The people in the IDP camps must endure dust storms in the dry season, mud in the rainy season and unimaginable filth all year round. Water is scarce and toilets are few. Residents are vulnerable to disease and abuse from promiscuity, squalor and inhumane conditions.[55]

Food Dependency. There is almost no self-sufficiency for people in the IDP camps. These agrarian people have no land to farm and no way to make money. How can they feed and care for their families?

They are almost totally dependent on outside agencies for food. Much of what they receive is yellow corn that comes from western nations, which does not taste the same as the white "maize" that was a past staple of Northern Uganda. One of my pastor friends told me, "The people just want to be out of these camps so they can go home and eat their own food."

It's no surprise that these victims become hostile about their conditions. Can you blame them? This hostility may often be turned toward one another. Desperation can cause a fierce scramble for goods when they arrive, resulting in fights and arguments breaking out among the citizens.

Many people try to scratch out small gardens in the areas along the roads that lead to and from the camps. But because they are so totally dependent on others, they sometimes can't afford to own even the basic tools necessary to grow even a little of their own food.

During one of our visits to the Pabbo IDP camp, a lady told us that it would be such a help to them if they could just get hoes so they could plant extra food. Do you know how much a hoe costs in Uganda? Three dollars! Only three dollars, yet tens of thousands of people can't afford to buy even one.

Danger. Because of the limited resources in the camps, many people—both adults and children—leave on a daily basis, walking miles out into the countryside in order to garden, find firewood or get water. This has significantly increased the chances of abduction.

Fourteen-year old Gladys Akello shared with me how she and her sister were abducted by the rebels when they went into the bush one day to collect firewood. "We were approached by five men, five gunmen. The gunmen took my sister, beat her thoroughly, and then we were taken home. From home we collected all the hens around and put them in the sack and I was made to carry those hens on my head. We moved around our area in Gulu District. I stayed in the bush for seven months." Gladys was finally able to find the strength and courage to escape and she found her way home … but she endured seven months of captivity and trauma, all because the simple task of gathering firewood made her easy prey for the rebels.

Health problems. The residents of these squalid camps often suffer from a variety of intestinal ailments, meningitis and sexually transmitted diseases, as well as the common cold and flu. Cholera outbreaks are also prevalent.

Uganda has been a model of success with its AIDS reduction efforts over the past 20 years, reducing its infection rate from 30 percent down to 6 percent.[56] But in the IDP camps, estimates are that the AIDS rates are as high as 15 to 20 percent. Uganda as a whole has made significant progress ... but AIDS is still a primary problem in the camps. Health centers have few drugs and little staff.

No education. Despite the government's policy of universal education throughout Uganda, large numbers of children in the North either do not attend school or attend classes where one teacher instructs far too many students. Some reports indicate as many as 300 students for every teacher in some classrooms.[57] I can only imagine how difficult it must be to keep control of a class that large! Finding teachers who will work in the IDP camps is very difficult, and at times, school is really nothing more than "child-sitting."

Few students continue their studies beyond primary school because of the high cost of secondary school fees. Hundreds of thousands of children can't go to school simply because they must help their families to survive. The dropout rate is high and there are few, if any, training or employment opportunities in the camps ... leaving young people bored and hopeless.

> "Most of the children in this camp were
> born here. They have known only the camp
> as their home."
>
> —Ugandan pastor in Gulu

Many young people who have been abducted by the LRA have completely missed their opportunity for education. Boys are too old or too emotionally scarred to go back to primary school. "Child mothers" must now care for their own babies and have no chance at an education. Nearly 250,000 children in Northern Uganda receive no education at all.[58]

Alcoholism. There is a great deal of idle time in the camps, which causes alcohol consumption to increase. People often sell the food they are given in order to buy alcohol. Many of the women have learned how to brew alcohol using corn provided by aid agencies, and they sell it as a way to earn money.[59] Needless to say ... this breeds additional levels of disorder and chaos in the IDP camps. Family violence and sexual abuse result. Although government soldiers are there for protection and to maintain the functionality of the camps, there is very little they can do when alcohol enters the mix.

IDP Camps at a Glance

- More than 1.7 million people are internally displaced.
- More than 200 camps house displaced people in Northern Uganda.
- Some individual camps hold more than 60,000 people.
- Over three quarters of displaced families have no access to land to farm.
- Nearly 70% of displaced families have no monetary income.
- 95% of displaced people in Northern Ugandan districts live in absolute poverty.
- 50% of Uganda's internally displaced people are children under age 15.

Source: Civil Society Organizations for Peace in Northern Uganda (CSOPNU)

Hopelessness. I don't know if any of us can begin to imagine the utter sense of hopelessness that permeates the IDP camps. Men, who are the heads of their families, have no way to provide for them, which causes a feeling of inadequacy. They are totally dependent on others. The boredom is overwhelming. Families have been torn apart and the self-respect of adults and children alike is destroyed. Emotional scars from so much death, suffering and upheaval are deep.

Violence. In many ways, each family must fend for itself to secure basic survival resources, as well as to shield one another from the horrors outside the camps' borders. The family structure is often a casualty of the civil strife and the IDP camps, where much domestic abuse occurs.[60] With the availability of alcohol, the threats of the LRA and general helplessness, it is no surprise that families break down. Children are abused, wives are raped and battered, and men fight each other. This breakdown in social structure is destroying any semblance of stability for the children.

The social and physical consequences of the war in Northern Uganda leave the citizens injured and distraught, with indelible marks on the psychological state of those in IDP camps.

In December 2005, the World Help team visited several IDP camps, including one that was home to 17,000 people. It was sobering when one of the pastors said, "Most of the children in this camp were born here. They have known only the camp as their home."

who's at fault?

Obviously, Joseph Kony and the LRA bear almost total responsibility for so many years of unimaginable pain and suffering for the people of Northern Uganda. Their terrorist practices and actions have wrought so much havoc, killed so many people and inflicted so much emotional grief on so many children and families.

Some people and organizations say that the government of Uganda bears some responsibility for "not acting fast enough" or "not providing enough resources." Some say that the United States and the West have not done enough to apply political pressure to bring an end to the war and the IDP camps.

Hindsight is always 20/20, and when we look back at the history of the situation in the North, it's easy to see where one course of action might have been better than another. But I think that it is far more constructive to look ahead at what can be done right now to help those most impacted by this tragedy—the children.

WHO REALLY CARES?

Ugandans and human rights workers say the war in Northern Uganda has received little notice from the rest of the world. In 2003, Jan Egeland, the United Nations Undersecretary-General for Humanitarian Affairs, told the BBC: "I cannot find any other part of the world that is having an emergency on the scale of Uganda that is getting so little international attention."[61]

The situation in the Darfur region of the Sudan has received far more international notice, even though it is of roughly the same magnitude as the Ugandan conflict in terms of human death and displacement. In fact, in October of 2005, "excess death rates in Northern Uganda [were] three times higher than those recorded in Darfur."[62]

Despite its location along the border with oil-rich Sudan, some say that Northern Uganda has no significant resources, and is therefore not a priority for the rest of the world ... or even the rest of Uganda. It is also part of a country generally hailed as an African success story. Since most of Uganda has seen an incredible turnaround in AIDS infection rates and great economic growth, why should they worry about a little disturbance up north?

Dr. Rima Salah, deputy executive director of UNICEF, said in an address to the congressional Human Rights Caucus in Washington that I attended: "What I saw in the faces and heard in the voices of these children was the total collapse of a secure environment. Children are bearing the brunt of hardship—they are brutalized and forced to endure hard labor, sexual exploitation and abuse. The past 20 years of conflict and its devastating impact on children must be addressed by joint efforts of the international community."[63]

But there are signs of hope. In the past three years, World Help and many other organizations have gotten involved and significantly increased the awareness of the Northern Uganda disaster among people in the United States.

The Ugandan government is open to the possibility of a negotiated settlement and resettling the IDP camp population. But the situation is still volatile. Despite reductions in the size of the LRA and periodic lapses in open warfare, "it is still capable of inflicting damage."

so what can we do?

"Africa's Friendliest Country" ...

"Uganda, Gifted by Nature" ...

Whatever the tourism slogan ... whatever the perception of Uganda as a whole, the reality is that its desperate people in the North need help—and lots of it! They need help from within Uganda and from without.

As I have reflected on all of the complex history, opinions and explanations of why this situation is as it is, as well as all the personal stories of tragedy that many courageous children have shared with me ... I have continually come back to one primary thought. Regardless of causes or fault, we *must* do something. We *must* do something to help the suffering people of Northern Uganda. We *must* do something to help the hundreds of thousands of Forgotten Children.

God has not called me or World Help to be involved in the politics or the processes of attempting to sway governments to do more. But from the first time I set foot in Gulu, God definitely called me to help in significant and tangible ways. He called me to reach out to hurting children ... to do something to help give them hope and a future.

The need is so enormous—almost a million Forgotten

Children.[64] My prayer was, "God, how do I start? What do you want me to do? How can one person really do something to make a difference in the lives of Uganda's Forgotten Children?"

photo journal

A normal day on the streets of Gulu, until thousands of children flood into the town seeking shelter from the LRA.

Hundreds of Forgotten Children sleep wherever they can find shelter, no matter the crowded conditions.

Internally Displaced Persons (IDP) camps are composed of mud huts, 10 feet in diameter, with as many as 15 family members crammed into a single hut. Plastic coverings have provided some additional shelter.

Thousands of people are forced to live in the squalor of IDP camps without adequate food, water or health services.

50% of Uganda's IDP camps consist of children under the age of 15.

Streams like this are the only substantial source of water at many of the IDP camps.

Ugandan military on patrol through the streets of Gulu.

A government official meets with Vernon Brewer and Alex Mitala in Lira to discuss the Forgotten Children crisis and how best to help these children.

More than 30,000 young boys and girls have died in the 20-year conflict between the Lord's Resistance Army and the Ugandan government.

"Night commuters" walk as far as eight miles to sleep on the streets, in bus parks or makeshift shelters of the towns. They are seeking safety for the night.

Skip Taylor, Chairman of World Help's Board of Directors, gets one-on-one time with some of the Forgotten Children at the Noah's Ark Shelter.

In the villages and camps at night, children are at risk for abduction by the violent Ugandan rebels looking for sex slaves and child soldiers.

As many as 40,000 children—some as young as 5 years old—leave their villages to take refuge in the towns of Northern Uganda each night.

On her first trip to Uganda, the Forgotten Children captured the heart of Mary Ellen Moomaw.

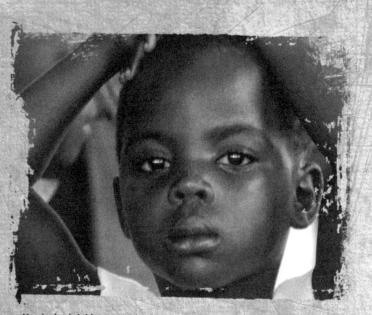

Hundreds of children roam the dirty Internally Displaced Persons camps. Some are clothed in rags; others have no clothes. Many of them are starving; some are dying from AIDS and other diseases.

More than 25,000 children, ages 7 to 17, have been abducted from towns and camps since the war started in 1986.

93

Children at the Adyel Good Samaritan Center in Lira wear shoes for the very first time.

Grace told Cody Surratt that she was abducted and raped by the LRA rebels and had a baby at the age of 12.

Josh Brewer becomes instant friends with some of the Forgotten Children in Gulu.

Vernon Brewer and Pastor Doyle Surratt met many of the Forgotten Children in Gulu, where the first idea of helping these children was born.

Gilbert Bukenya, the Vice President of Uganda, welcomes a World Help medical team at a bush clinic near Kampala.

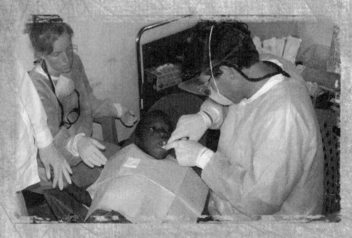

World Help medical team provides dental care to children at the Good Samaritan Children's Home in Kampala.

Vernon Brewer and son, Josh, visit with Vice President of Uganda, Professor Gilbert Balibaseka Bukenya, in his home to discuss the strategy for the Good Samaritan Children's Centers.

Michael Tait of DC Talk recorded with Children of the World to help raise awareness of the Forgotten Children of Uganda.

Ben Moomaw and Alex Mitala are encouraged at the progress made at the Pabbo Good Samaritan Children's Center.

Nikki Hart listening to the unbelievable stories of some of the Forgotten Children.

98

Vernon Brewer and Tom Thompson take the opportunity to spend time with the children at the Tegwana Good Samaritan Children's Center in Gulu.

Nearly 2.4 million children under the age of 15 have lost one or both parents to HIV/AIDS. They have no one to care for them.

5

hope for the children

" But the needy will

not always be forgotten,

nor the hope of the

afflicted ever perish."

—Psalm 9:18

T he more children I met in Gulu and the more stories I heard, the more I knew that God brought me to this place, at this particular time, for a specific purpose. With all my heart, I felt He wanted World Help to do something significant to help these suffering Forgotten Children.

But there are so many children in Northern Uganda, so many horrific stories, and so much that must be done … it's overwhelming. Where do you start? With a single child.

That realization was never more real to me than the night I visited Noah's Ark, a shelter where several hundred of the Forgotten Children were sleeping in tents. Nearly 4,000 had trekked to Gulu that particular evening. Some were sleeping at a government safe compound, some on the floor of a bus park, and some just out in the open.

Parents didn't know if their children would make it home safely the next day, while children didn't know if their parents would be there when they returned.

I stood next to our ministry partner, Alex Mitala, watching over 300 children as they sang, praised God and said their prayers. It hit me all over again that this is their daily experience … one which has been indelibly printed on my mind and heart. When I glanced over at Alex, he was weeping. He said, "These atrocities must stop!"

It was difficult for either of us to speak. The enormity of the problem weighed heavily on my mind. I asked permission to stay and spend more time with the children.

One day a man was walking along the beach when he noticed a figure in the distance. As he got closer, he realized the figure was that of a boy picking something up and gently throwing it into the ocean. Approaching the boy he asked, "What are you doing?"

The youth replied, "Throwing the starfish back into the ocean. The sun is up and the tide is going out. If I don't throw them back, they'll die."

"Son," the man said, "don't you realize there are miles and miles of beach and hundreds of starfish? You can't possibly make a difference."

After listening politely, the boy bent down, picked up another starfish, and threw it into the surf. Then smiling at the man, he said, "I made a difference for that one."

—Adapted from "The Star Thrower"
by Loren Eiseley

My heart broke as I was able to tuck those young boys in and pray with them. As I looked into the face of each child, I began to understand that our heavenly Father knows each one.

He formed and created them individually, with unique talents, gifts and desires. When God looks at the problem in Northern Uganda, He doesn't see a mass of bodies or a sea of faces. He sees Grace. He cries for Moses. Every single boy and girl is precious in His eyes ... and to save even one is worth any price.

> "The Spirit himself testifies with our spirit that we are God's children. Now if we are children, then we are heirs—heirs of God and co-heirs with Christ."
>
> —Romans 8:16-17

As long as I live ... I'll never forget that night when the Forgotten Children became real to me.

a vision... a plan

Later on that trip, I met with Alex and other pastors in the region to pray and discuss a way to meet the needs of these very real children. They came together from all over Northern Uganda ... some even had to ride a bus all night to get there.

When we all sat down and I looked into their faces, I knew there was no way I could send them home empty-handed. It was so obvious that they all had a strong compassion. They were sacrificing their time out of love.

One pastor told me, "It's not that we don't care about these children. We desperately want to help them … but our people are so poor … we just don't have the resources. We have the compassion, we just don't have the money."

I prayed and asked God for a strategy that would be culturally sensitive and would allow those pastors to meet this great need. I wasn't interested in making our presence known or getting credit for anything we would do. All I truly wanted was to provide the resources these pastors needed to take care of these children.

When we first began to talk to the pastors about what we could do to help, we suggested that they might consider starting small orphanages. The church could "take in" orphans and provide for their care, since they had no parents.

But the pastors told us that this wouldn't be a good idea. They said that the Acholi people value family ties and caring for family very highly, and that it was culturally very insensitive to even suggest that someone outside a child's extended family would be given the responsibility to care for the child. They told us that no matter what happened to a child's parents, the extended family—uncles, aunts, grandparents, cousins—would always think it was their responsibility to care for that child.

In the same conversation, the concept of children's centers was born. God was already at work! The area pastors had developed a simple yet effective strategy that would help the children, but would also be culturally appropriate for the Acholi people.

These pastors identified 10 churches in Northern Uganda whose buildings were only used a few hours each week. They wanted these buildings to house havens for the children—what they would call Good Samaritan Children's Centers.

We chose the term "children's centers" because we saw that these pastors and their churches could be central "coordination points" for providing a variety of resources to needy children.

> "It's not that we don't care about these children. We desperately want to help them ... but our people are so poor ... we just don't have the resources."
>
> —A pastor in Northern Uganda

Each church would choose 50 of the neediest children to be helped. The pastor and his wife would serve as the directors and coordinators of that particular center. The pastors and leaders of these churches live day in and day out in the middle of the suffering that so many children must endure. They are in a unique position to know how to best meet the needs of the children. They are respected in their towns and they speak the languages. And they know the government officials, the camp commanders, the military leaders and the school officials.

God has given each of these committed pastors a unique vision and compassion about how to give the children in their own communities hope and a better future. Our support would help them provide food, clothing, medicine, educational assistance, as well as trauma and grief counseling. At the same time, they would share the Gospel message of Christ and put His love into action. How could I say "no"?

Alex and the other pastors moved quickly. When I returned to Uganda only a few months later, they had already identified the children and were ready to start.

Each Good Samaritan Children's Center would cost $39,000 for one year. So our immediate goal was to raise a minimum of $390,000 to get all 10 centers up and running for at least the first year. The money would provide for structural improvements to the existing buildings that would house the centers. It would also allow for each center to be fully furnished and cover the cost of all utilities, salaries (for cooks, academic tutors and supervisors) and school fees. The children would also be provided with daily meals, medical care, grief counseling, uniforms and clothing, scholastic materials and Bible lessons.

The pastors shared with me that if they did not have the financial resources in the next 60 days, they would miss the deadline for registering the children in boarding school. I knew that we could not possibly wait another year to help these children begin their educations. We had to act immediately.

I told the pastors, "We don't have the money, but I will go home and cast the vision for these Forgotten Children. Somehow, by faith, in the next 60 days we will trust God to meet this need." Then I said, "Our job is to work hard and cast the vision ... your role in this partnership is to pray."

And did those pastors ever pray! When we had finished petitioning God that day, I didn't know how we were going to do it, but I knew somehow God was going to make it happen.

a miraculous answer to prayer

Within days of returning home, God began answering our prayers.

A group of 55 members from a church in Cypress, California, had spent time in Uganda on one of World Help's short-term mission trips. Key leaders from the church accompanied me on a flight to Gulu. They saw the need firsthand, and their hearts were broken. When they returned home, their pastor shared the urgent need with the congregation.

In that one weekend, the church raised enough funds to provide for four centers for a year. It was incredible!

So we only needed six more.

I arrived home from Uganda on a Friday night and had to leave early the next morning for a speaking engagement at a church in Columbus, Ohio.

When I spoke on Saturday night, much to my surprise, they presented me with a check to provide for one children's center for a year. They had heard about the need and had been raising funds for several weeks. Later that night, I received a phone call from a businessman who was in the service that night. He told me he was sending another check in order to make their gift enough to provide for two centers.

The next day I was sitting in the Columbus airport, once again heading home, not yet recuperated from the Uganda trip and from speaking three times over the weekend. But I was pumped—I had funds in hand for two additional children's centers. At that moment, my cell phone rang ... it was my daughter, Nikki. She was with the *Children of the World* choir at a church in Myrtle Beach, South Carolina.

She said, "Dad, you are not going to believe it. This

morning the children sang and showed the Forgotten Children video (filmed during our first trip to Gulu depicting this horrific situation). The church took an offering … it was enough for four centers!" At first I thought there was static in the line, so I asked her to repeat what she said. That was the single largest offering in the history of World Help.

When I hung up the phone, I did the math in my head and sat there in disbelief. We now had enough money to start all 10 centers. It didn't take 60 days … it only took six!

I realized the power of those Ugandan pastors' prayers and that God was honoring our joint partnership efforts to help the Forgotten Children. Unbelievable!

ONLY THE BEGINNING

Since that trip in 2005 when my Ugandan pastor friends shared their vision and their strategy with us, so much has been accomplished. Not only have we raised enough funds to provide for 10 Good Samaritan Children's Centers for the first year, but we've also raised money to start a Good Samaritan Center for Trade Skills, a place where 220 older children can receive vocational training. There are four children's centers in or near the town of Gulu, two in the town of Lira, two in the town of Kitgum and two near the town of Pader. The trade center is located in Gulu Town.

All of the Good Samaritan Children's Centers have the following strategies in common:

- Each center provides for the needs of 50 children.
- Each center helps the neediest children— young children and teenagers, in camps or villages, who were orphaned when either one or both parents died because of violence or AIDS.
- Each center ensures a Christ-centered focus for all of the activities and programs they undertake. They show these children the love of Jesus on a consistent basis, week in and week out.
- Each center provides appropriate educational resources, given the unique needs and situation of each of the children. Education is the key to helping each child escape from hopelessness and poverty.
- Each center makes effective use of the resources the churches do have—the buildings and the members of the church who so desperately want to help.

Each Good Samaritan Children's Center is also uniquely designed to meet specific needs that are prevalent in the villages and IDP camps near the church. Some are functioning as "day care centers." The children come to the centers in the morning and leave late in the afternoon. The centers provide them with three meals a day, basic primary school education and the love of Christ. This is the wisest approach for needy children whose families or caretakers moved permanently to one of the four main towns to escape the violence.

Other centers provide primary boarding school education for the younger children. There are a number of Christian boarding schools in Northern Uganda that are working with our centers. The pastors regularly check up on the progress of the children, and the children stay with the pastors and their churches during holiday times. This is best for children who live in IDP camps.

Some of the centers help teenagers by providing resources for them to attend existing vocational training programs in fields such as welding, carpentry, masonry, sewing and hair care. This is a good option for teenagers who have only a seventh-grade education or less. Vocational training at or near the center helps the neediest of teenagers, who have been robbed of an education and cannot qualify for conventional vocational programs.

We are in the process of establishing three additional Good Samaritan Centers for Trade Skills that will ultimately train hundreds of young people every year.

But despite the success of these centers, I must tell

you—World Help cannot stop here. We are not going to help the Forgotten Children for only one year and then abandon them. Our strategy to help the children is both immediate and long-term. God has called World Help to play a part both in providing help to these children now and in giving them hope for a future.

Our long-term strategy is two-fold:

1. **Provide enough funds to support the Children's Centers and Vocational Training Center(s) for three years, or until they become self-sustaining.** We must raise $1.6 million to sustain the 10 Good Samaritan Children's Centers and the four Good Samaritan Centers for Trade Skills for at least three years. During this time, we will have provided hope for nearly 4,000 young people. There is much more to be done and we are in this for the long haul. Just imagine the impact we will have made on thousands of children and the lives that will be changed because of it!

2. **Find sponsors for all of the children in the Good Samaritan Children's Centers through our Child Sponsorship**

Program. Our desire is to find enough sponsors in the next three years to provide for the long-term support of the centers. For only $24 a month, a sponsor can help a Forgotten Child experience God's love in such a way that they commit their lives to His service. Christ-centered children's havens will play a significant part in raising up the next generation of Christian pastors, church planters, teachers, doctors and nurses throughout Uganda. And we trust that God will continue to provide for these centers for the first three years in the same miraculous ways He has provided for their beginning.

This strategy has opened up even more doors to helping the people of Uganda. During one visit to Gulu, I was privileged to meet with the Vice President, Professor Gilbert Balibaseka Bukenya. I told the Vice President of our strategy in Northern Uganda for 10 Good Samaritan Children's Centers and he thanked me for being part of the solution to the problem. He also shared with me how we could further help Uganda in a way that is very close to his heart.

Before Vice President Bukenya entered politics, he was a medical doctor. A few years ago during his campaign, he found a seriously ill girl in his political district, not far from his home. But there was not a hospital or clinic for miles around. So he put her in his car and drove her all the way to the nearest hospital. But he didn't make it in time— she died.

Bukenya was so shaken by the experience that he went to the village and built a medical clinic with his own money. He is still personally funding the staffing of the clinic. He asked if I would help provide more clinics in the bush, and I promised him that we would provide as many as we could with the help of our friends back in the States.

After I returned home, I shared this need with my good friend Michael Tait of DC Talk. Mike was moved by the suffering of the people of Uganda and wanted to get involved. He is now partnering with us to provide as many medical clinics as we can in the neediest areas of Africa.

Not only will these clinics provide the medical attention that the adults so desperately need, but they will also ultimately help hundreds of thousands of children that have been innocently infected with HIV/AIDS, various sicknesses and other preventable diseases. But most importantly, we will have the opportunity to share the love of Christ with every person and family treated in the clinics.

6
making
a DIFFERENCE

"Some day when you stand before God and He asks, 'Did you know about what was going on in Northern Uganda?' What will you say? If He asks, 'Did you know children were being murdered, raped and abducted? What did you do?'"

—U. S. Senator
Sam Brownback

In the months since we first started this God-sized project, our partners have reached out and helped literally hundreds of formerly Forgotten Children— children who just last year were making the arduous trek each night into Gulu and other cities for safety … children who were trying to find enough food to survive in the IDP camps … children who were abducted, brutalized and forced to kill by the LRA.

Hundreds of these boys and girls are enrolled in schools or existing vocational training programs and benefit from the tutoring, counseling and Bible lessons of the 10 children's centers. Another several hundred will be taught to sew, weld or work in the hair care trade each year at the Good Samaritan Centers for Trade Skills. These children, who were helpless and without hope, are learning to become self-sufficient … they are beginning to have hope for the future. And most importantly, they are learning that Jesus Christ loves and cares about them.

Can you see them?

Can you see Grace, shaking with sobs and traumatized by watching her infant murdered in front of her eyes … now lifting those same eyes up to the Lord? Can you see Moses, distraught over being forced to pull the trigger and kill his own brother … now using his hands to learn a trade? I can. I have seen them. And I can tell you that God is faithful to redeem what was lost.

119

I have gone back to Northern Uganda with members of the World Help staff several times since our partners started the Good Samaritan Children's Centers and the first Center for Trade Skills, and the progress they have made is astounding. God is truly working through them to reach the Forgotten Children of Uganda.

Anya Ariamo shared her story with me and my team as we were sitting on a hill overlooking a Good Samaritan Children's Center in Gulu.

Gesturing towards the children playing around us, she said, "I have a daughter. She's one of the children in this center. I've got five more children. My husband was killed by LRA rebels ... his body was left to rot in the jungle."

Like many other wives in Gulu, Anya has been left with the full responsibility for her children—a daunting task in a place where food is scarce and safety uncertain. "I am now the one taking care of these children. I do not have the strength, the resources, to keep these children, more especially concerning their education ... I find difficulty in getting food. I rent a small, grass-roofed mud hut. We do not have enough food."

It was taking all of Anya's strength just to keep her family together and provide for them each day. Now, with the help of the children's center, Anya has hope: "God is helping us ... I thank God that He saved me so that today I got life because of His love for me.

"I can see that there are people that have given

another, I found that I've forgotten what I've passed through. I get comfort from the center ... through our life we get encouragement."

These are only three of the hundreds of stories of children whose lives are being restored because of the work of our partners in Uganda and the faithfulness of God.

Ben Moomaw, World Help's Vice President of International Ministries, recently returned from visiting the centers and shared this incredible news:

Overall, it's amazing how well they've been able to organize this whole program, given that it's basically in a war zone. I got to see many of the children at the centers. It was incredible to see the difference three or four months of someone caring has made in the lives of these kids.

I also got a chance to meet with the families of some of the children in one of the IDP camps, all of whom were astonished at the positive changes they've seen in their kids after just one term of school. We're making a big difference in a lot of young lives ... it's incredible what God has given us the privilege of doing together for His kingdom in Uganda in the last few years.

I spent a busy nine days visiting nine of the 10 Good Samaritan Children's Centers. It was a school holiday time while I was there, so I got a chance to see many of the children who were home from their boarding schools.

At the Cereleno Center in Gulu, I visited with a number of older kids that we'd seen for the first time in December 2005, before they were able to start their vocational training and/or high school classes. One girl in particular stands out. Her name is Gladys Akello. When we interviewed her in December, she told us that when she was abducted by the LRA she was forced to kill two people. She was a sullen, sad, troubled young mother. She seemed absolutely devoid of hope. But when I saw Gladys this time, she was a totally changed young lady—her countenance was totally different. She had such a big smile on her face—so much that I almost didn't recognize her. She is now a student at Gulu Central High School and doing great.

During the visit, our partner Alex Mitala was encouraging all of the kids toward achievement by telling them he expected to see many of them become teachers, doctors, nurses and the like. Gladys spoke up, adding an emphatic, "And President!" to Alex's list. What an incredible indication of the hope that Gladys now has!

I also visited the Pabbo Internally Displaced Persons camp, about 20 miles north of Gulu. It is the largest of the refugee camps in Uganda—over 63,000 people crammed into acres and acres of small thatch-roofed huts so close together that I could hardly walk between them. It is one of the dirtiest places I've ever been. So many children had only rags for clothing. I had a soft drink with me and quickly learned that the bottle cap alone would be a prized

possession for any of these children. That
realization really struck home to me.

In the middle of this vast helplessness
and poverty was a small church building
that is home to the Pabbo Good Samaritan
Children's Center. It provides for 50 children
from the camp who are now in school at two
different Christian boarding schools. I
spent a couple of hours visiting with the
kids (who were home from school for a
holiday), with many of their parents and
guardians and with Pastor Armstrong and
his wife, who are the leaders of the center.

One mother said, "Before, our children
lived like pigs. They just ran around all
day—we didn't see them from morning until
night, and they were unruly and wouldn't
do what we said. Since they have been at
school, they are totally changed. They are
happy, they do their work, and they respect
us. We almost didn't recognize them when
they came home."

It is obvious that the Good Samaritan
Children's Center in Pabbo, and likewise

the other centers I visited, are providing immediate, substantial help and hope to the children in their care.

While I was in Lira, I visited with a large group of children and parents from both of the Good Samaritan Children's Centers there. Again, it was so encouraging to hear and see that these young kids (ages 4 through 7), who are attending a local Christian school in Lira, are being transformed.

I sat for about 30 minutes in the dirt under a tree outside of the Boke Center in Lira just playing with kids. I drew pictures of animals in the dirt with a stick and was amazed at how the kids could identify in English what most of the animals were (even though I'm a very poor wildlife artist). They knew their ABCs and could count very well. Just think ... none of these children had a shred of education before February. It was great to see so many happy smiling faces—children with life in their eyes!

When Ben returned from his trip, moved by the continuing tragedy, but motivated by the incredible progress, he reminded me, "One of the most important things we have to do with these centers is to be involved with them for the long haul—to stick with the kids we're helping until they finish their educations, not just help for a year or two or three."

We must sustain the 10 Good Samaritan Children's Centers and the four Good Samaritan Centers for Trade Skills. So our work has just begun.

compassion in action

Supporting these centers is an opportunity to put hands and feet to the compassion of Christ. Together, we can make a difference for the Forgotten Children. We are called by Christ to make an impact on those who are in desperate need.

"And if you spend yourselves in behalf of the hungry and satisfy the needs of the oppressed, then your light will rise in the darkness, and your night will become like the noonday."

—Isaiah 58:10

"The difference between an ordinary Christian and a deeply committed one is that the ordinary Christian gets emotional, while the deeply committed Christian gets involved."

—K. G. McMillan

Recently, I attended a congressional Human Rights Caucus in Washington, D.C., that focused on the children. There were several hundred participants and representatives from both governmental and nongovernmental organizations. I also sat in on a two-hour congressional briefing as the wars and atrocities of Northern Africa were discussed.

U. S. Senator Sam Brownback made a statement during the event that impacted me. He said, "Some day when you stand before God and He asks, 'Did you know about what was going on in Northern Uganda?' What will you say? If He asks, 'Did you know children were being murdered, raped and abducted? What did you do?'" Then he said, "Will you tell God, 'I watched TV, I read magazines, I surfed the internet,' is that what you will say?" He added, "If you had known about the Holocaust while it was happening, would you have done something? If we don't do

"'... For I was hungry and you gave me
something to eat, I was thirsty and you
gave me something to drink, I was a
stranger and you invited me in, I needed
clothes and you clothed me, I was sick
and you looked after me, I was in prison
and you came to visit me.'

Then the righteous will answer him,
'Lord, when did we see you hungry and
feed you, or thirsty and give you
something to drink? When did we see
you a stranger and invite you in, or
needing clothes and clothe you? When
did we see you sick or in prison and go
to visit you?'

The King will reply, 'I tell you the
truth, whatever you did for one of the
least of these brothers of mine, you
did for me.'"

—Matthew 25:31-40

something about Uganda, people will die!"[65]

These hurting children in Uganda need us!

As Christians, we cannot leave it to others to save these hurting little ones. We must be the ones to step up to the challenge and take the lead by acting in compassion. We can no longer allow these children to be forgotten.

You can get personally involved today.

Together, we can offer the resources these Ugandan pastors so desperately need to provide food, clothing and shelter for the Forgotten Children and to offer them an education. Most importantly, through these Good Samaritan Centers, the children will see the love and compassion of Christ in action. They will learn that Jesus loves them and has provided an eternal hope for them.

And because people in these communities and surrounding areas will see how the children are being helped, they will want to know more. What a tremendous opportunity these pastors will have to share Jesus Christ with them as well!

The story of the Forgotten Children is definitely tragic … but there is hope in the midst of despair. We can make a difference in the lives of children like Grace and Moses … one at a time.

Please do not forget about these children. I know I never will … and I hope you won't either. The Forgotten Children desperately need our help … they need a lot of help. Everyone can do something. Everyone can help.

Will you do something? Will you tell their story to your family, friends and everyone you know ... so they won't forget either? Will you pray that God will stop this insanity ... and save these children? Will you help us ... TODAY?

"If you can accomplish only one thing today, tomorrow or in your lifetime ... let it be that you save the life of a child."

—Vernon Brewer

GET INVOLVED... TODAY!

If the tragic story of the desperate children in Northern Uganda has made a profound impact on your heart, you can give the Forgotten Children help and hope right now. Put your compassion into action by getting involved in one or more of the following ways:

PRAY. The Forgotten Children and our ministry need your prayers. According to James 5:16, "The prayer of a righteous man is powerful and effective." Your prayers will make a difference. Please pray for the children of Northern Uganda. Pray for peace. Pray that God will give wisdom to the leaders of the nation and the world in dealing with this humanitarian tragedy. And pray that He will use the ministry of World Help to make a difference in the lives of hurting children.

GIVE. World Help must raise $1.6 million to sustain the 10 Good Samaritan Children's Centers and the four Good Samaritan Centers for Trade Skills for at least three years. Your gift will literally help save lives as we provide shelter, food, clothing, medical care, grief counseling, educational materials and life-changing Bible lessons. Or, if you want to connect with the children of Uganda on a more personal level, you can become a child sponsor. You can make a commitment today to provide for a child for an entire year, through our **Child Sponsorship Program.**

SHARE. The more caring friends like you who get involved in the tragedy of the Forgotten Children, the better chance they have for survival. I urge you to share the story of these children. You can also request a FREE DVD, *Into Africa … The Compelling Story of the Forgotten Children*. Shot on location in Northern Uganda, this gripping DVD will take you into the world of these young victims as you see firsthand the phenomenon of the "night commuters." You will meet Grace, Moses and other children who live this nightmare. Not only will viewing this DVD be a moving and emotional experience for you, it is also a great tool to tell the story of the Forgotten Children to your friends and family, church groups and others. **To request your free DVD or find out how you can help, log onto www.theforgottenchildren.com or call 1-800-541-6691.**

Together, we can save these children … one hurting boy or girl at a time.

With your help, they will not be forgotten for long.

"But the needy will not always be forgotten, nor the hope of the afflicted ever perish."
                                        —*Psalm 9:18*

RECERENCES

1   J. Carter Johnson, "Deliver Us from Kony," *Christianity Today*, Jan. 2006:32.

2   "Northern Uganda: Humanitarian Response to Crisis Still a Failure," *Refugees International Bulletin* 27 Feb. 2006.

3   "Northern Uganda: Humanitarian Response."

4   Priya Abraham, "One Dark Night," *World* 12 Nov. 2005, 16 Mar. 2006 http://www.worldmag.com/articles/11258.

5   "Understanding the War," Uganda Conflict Action Network report published as part of the Congressional Human Rights Caucus, Washington, D.C. 8-9 Mar. 2006.

6   "Uganda abductions," BBC News 4 June 2004, 9 June 2006 http://www.bbc.co.uk/radio4/womanshour/02_02_04/wednesday/info3.shtml

7   "2006 Report on the global AIDS epidemic," UNAIDS May 2006, 11 July 2006 http://data.unaids.org/pub/GlobalReport/2006/2006_GR_ANN1U-Z_en.pdf.

8   "Real Voices: Uganda's 'night commuters' live in shadow of fear," *AlertNet* 11 Aug. 2005, 30 Apr. 2006 http://www.alertnet.org/thefacts/reliefresources/112376984032.htm.

9   The Rt. Rev. Macleord Baker Ochola II, "The Crisis in Northern Uganda — Issues of Grave Concern," LaTrobe University 19 Mar. 2003, 9 June 2006 http://www.latrobe.edu.au/african/ARIfile/OcholaCrisis.html.

10 *Children of Uganda Homepage*, 28 Mar. 2006 http://childrenofuganda.org/.

11 "Northern Uganda: Humanitarian Response."

12 "World Briefing | Africa: Uganda: Children Drowned, Army Says." *New York Times* 18 July 2003, 18 Mar. 2006 http://query.nytimes.com/gst/fullpage.html?res=9B0DE2DC103CF93BA25754C0A9659C8B63&pagewanted.

13 "The Scars of Death: Children Abducted by the Lord's Resistance Army in Uganda," Human Rights Watch, 1 Sept. 1997, 12 Feb. 2006 http://www.hrw.org/reports97/uganda/.

14 Ochola.

15 Emily Wax, "In Uganda, a Fresh Start for Former Child Fighters," *Washington Post* Foreign Service, 13 Mar. 2006: A9.

16 "Northern Uganda: Humanitarian Response."

17 Dr. Rima Salah, address, Congressional Human Rights Caucus, Washington, D.C., 9 Mar. 2006.

18 "UNICEF Humanitarian Action: Uganda in 2006," UNICEF report published as part of the Congressional Human Rights Caucus, Washington, D.C., 8-9 Mar. 2006: 88.

19 Johnson 36.

20 "Bellamy urges attention on Uganda's displaced people crisis; Calls on LRA to release children," press release, UNICEF 25 May 2004, 14 June 2006 http://www.unicef.org/media/media_21136.html.

21 "The Shocking Story George Clooney Has to Tell," *Oprah Winfrey Show*, ABC, 27 Apr. 2006.

22 Johnson 37.

23 Johnson 37.

24 Johnson 31.

25 Carolyn Davis, "Jennifer's Journey," *Philadelphia Enquirer* 8 Feb.

2006, 18 Mar. 2006 http://www.philly.com/mld/inquirer/news/
special_packages/jennifer/13822954.htm.

26 "Real Voices."

27 "Real Voices."

28 "Real Voices."

29 "Real Voices."

30 Gilbert M. Khadiagala, "The Role of the Acholi Religious Leaders
Peace Initiative (ARLPI) in Peace Building in Northern Uganda,"
appendix to USAID report *The Effectiveness of Civil Society
Initiatives in Controlling Violent Conflicts and Building Peace: A
Study of Three Approaches in the Greater Horn of Africa*, Greater
Horn of Africa Peace Building Project (Washington, D.C.:
Management Systems International, 2001), 22 Feb. 2006
http://pdf.dec.org/pdf_docs/PNACY566.pdf.

31 Khadiagala.

32 Khadiagala.

33 "Joseph Kony," *Wikipedia* 22 Feb. 2006
<http://en.wikipedia.org/wiki/Joseph_Kony>.

34 Christopher Hitchens, "Childhood's End," *Vanity Fair* 9 Jan.
2006, 22 Feb. 2006 http://www.vanityfair.com/commentary/
content/printables/060109roco03.

35 Johnson 31.

36 Hitchens.

37 Hitchens.

38 Sam Farmar, "I will use the Ten Commandments to Liberate
Uganda," TimesOnline 28 June 2006 http://www.timesonline.
co.uk/article/0,,3-2246914.html.

137

39   Courtney Lancaster, "Child Soldiers," *World* 12 Nov. 2005, 16
     Mar. 2006 http://www.worldmag.com/articles/11258.

40   Khadiagala.

41   Khadiagala.

42   Johnson 35.

43   Rory E. Anderson, Fortunate Sewankambo and Kathy Vandergrift,
     "Pawns of Politics: Children, Conflict and Peace in Northern
     Uganda," 2004 World Vision report, 9 Mar. 2006
     http://www.worldvision.ca/home/media/UgandaPawnsOfPolitics 37

44   Anderson 37.

45   Johnson 35.

46   "Understanding the War."

47   Johnson 30.

48   Hitchens.

49   "Understanding the War."

50   Johnson 32.

51   Johnson 32.

52   Wax A9.

53   Anderson 4.

54   Anderson 17.

55   "UGANDA: IDP Camps, No Home Away From Home," UN Office
     for the Coordination of Humanitarian Affairs, 9 June 2005, 30 Mar.
     2006 http://www.irinnews.org/S_report.asp?ReportID=47571.

56 "Strategies: Youth Ministry," Building Uganda, 12 June 2006
building-uganda.org./youthskills.html.

57 "Key Facts after 20 years of war in northern Uganda," Civil
Society Organizations for Peace in Northern Uganda fact sheet
published as part of the Congressional Human Rights Caucus,
Washington, D.C., 8-9 Mar. 2006.

58 "Key Facts."

59 Michelle Brown and Kavita Shukla, "Inadequate Response to
Protection Crisis in Northern Uganda," Refugees International
12 Dec. 2004, 20 Feb. 2006 http://www.refugeesinternational.
org/content/article/detail/4677/?.

60 Brown and Shukla.

61 "Understanding the War."

62 "Key Facts."

63 "Dr. Rima Salah.

64 The 1 million Forgotten Children include the more than 900,000
children living in IDP camps (Salah 1), the 30,000 who have died
as a result of violence or disease brought on by the war (Johnson
32), the more than 25,000 children who have been abducted
("Understanding the War"), and the 40,000 night commuters
(Abraham).

65 U.S. Senator Sam Brownback (KS), statement during a
Congressional Human Rights Committee briefing on the wars
and atrocities of Northern Africa in Washington, D.C., 8-9
Mar. 2006.

aBOUT THE auThOR

"Every day, I try to live my life in such a way that I accomplish at least one thing that will outlive me and last for eternity."

—Vernon Brewer,
Personal Mission Statement

 **VERNON BREWER** is the founder and president of World Help, a non-profit, nondenominational Christian organization that was founded to meet the spiritual and physical needs of hurting people around the world.

His incredible life experiences, combined with his passion for the unreached peoples of the world, make Vernon an energetic and compassionate leader. His strategic thinking and emphasis on partnership have breathed new life into the mission world and provided innovative ways to partner together and accomplish more for the Kingdom of God.

He has conducted international evangelistic campaigns and rallies in over 50 foreign countries worldwide, as well as numerous leadership training conferences in Uganda, China, India, Nepal, Burma, Romania, and

Russia. In addition, Vernon has personally taken over 4,000 people to the mission field.

He is the first graduate of Liberty University (1973) where he also served 10 years as Dean of Students and Vice President of Student Affairs. Vernon has survived a major struggle with cancer, undergoing 18 surgeries and 18 months of chemotherapy. His personal testimony has been a source of encouragement to many people facing difficult situations.

why woRLD heLp?

As believers, we are commanded by God to love others and share the hope of Jesus Christ. Founded in 1991, World Help is a nonprofit, nondenominational Christian organization that exists to fulfill the Great Commission and the Great Commandment through partnering, training, helping and serving, especially in the unreached areas of the world.

This is accomplished through four pillars of ministry—humanitarian aid, church planting, child sponsorship and Bible distribution

Since our founding, World Help has touched over 58 countries through our ministries. We have seen and responded to the spiritual and humanitarian needs of people groups around the world. This is how we offer help and hope:

Humanitarian Aid. God loves and cares about suffering people. And if we share God's heart, we must see the world through His eyes … a world in need. Hunger, war, famine, disease and natural disaster create a worldwide climate of suffering that most of us cannot begin to comprehend.

World Help has seen firsthand the incredible suffering and hardships that people around the world endure every day of their lives. It is our desire to meet the physical needs of hurting people around the world and in so doing ... earn the right to be heard!

58 Countries We Have Helped:

Afghanistan	Laos
Albania	Liberia
Argentina	Malawi
Austria	Mexico
Bangladesh	Moldova
Bolivia	Morocco
Bosnia	Myanmar
Brazil	Nepal
China	Nicaragua
Cuba	Nigeria
D.R. Congo	Papua New
Ecuador	Guinea
Egypt	Peru
El Salvador	Philippines
France	Romania
Gambia	Russia
Guatemala	Rwanda
Haiti	Sierra Leone
Honduras	Somalia
Hungary	South Africa
India	Sudan
Indonesia	Thailand
Iraq	Trinidad
Iran	Uganda
Jamaica	Ukraine
Kenya	United Kingdom
Kosovo	United States
Kazakhstan	Vietnam
Lebanon	Zambia
Lithuania	

With the support of individuals, churches, organizations and medical facilities, World Help has shipped over 100 ocean-going containers and distributed critically needed humanitarian aid worldwide at an estimated value of $55 million.

Establish Churches. *"Go and make disciples of all nations"* was the last command Jesus gave His disciples. Jesus did not command us to do the impossible, nor did He command us to go to the ends of the earth with His Gospel if He did not expect us to obey. However, today there are still entire groups of people who have never heard of Jesus Christ.

Church-planting movements are the key to evangelizing the least-reached peoples of the world. Utilizing national church planters, effective church-planting movements penetrate entire people groups with the Gospel. It is the vision of World Help to help plant indigenous, reproducing churches where no churches currently exist. To date, God has allowed us to plant over 31,000 churches in the unreached areas of the world.

Love Children. Millions of people around the world suffer hardship, hunger and disease. But those who suffer the most are the children. They endure unimaginable living conditions on a daily basis without any hope of a better future.

In the face of these great needs one can feel overwhelmed. World Help's Child Sponsorship Program was born out of the desire to "change the world … one child at a time." World Help has provided over 18,000 sponsorships for children in desperate need around the world. A sponsor can provide a child with the basic necessities … food, clothing, medical attention and educational opportunities. Most importantly, these children receive the message that God loves them and has a special plan for their lives.

Provide Bibles. World Help has witnessed an immense hunger for God's Word all around the world. Thousands risk their lives every day for the sake of the Gospel. Pastors, church leaders, Christians of all nationalities beg us to provide them with Bibles … and we can help them!

The Bible is the most powerful tool God has given us to reach the souls of lost people throughout our world. It is the most important resource we can place in any believer's hand.

World Help was founded on fulfilling this most basic and desperate need. Since inception, we have printed and distributed more than 8 million Bibles, New Testaments and other pieces of Christian literature to places where they are needed the most.

"Thousands have partnered with World Help and God has allowed us to see countless lives miraculously changed ... thousands of churches planted in places where there were none ... children receiving help and hope through sponsorships ... and millions of Bibles provided to those who have never seen a Bible, much less owned one. Together, we are committed to sharing Christ's love, His hope and His peace with the unreached people of this world."

—Vernon Brewer

We are committed to:

- Authentic Relationships and Teamwork
- Fanatical Attention to Quality and Detail
- Working with Passion and Enthusiasm
- Always Doing What is Right
- Accomplishing God-Sized Tasks that Last for Eternity

World Help is also committed to faithful stewardship of funds entrusted to us by donors. We promise to use your gifts wisely and effectively in Christ's name and provide information, a network of international contacts, and financial and ministry accountability for each mission project in which we participate. World Help strives to keep overhead costs to a minimum using only 9% for the administration of our various projects. All gifts designated for specific projects are used as designated. To ensure our financial accountability to you, World Help is a member of the Evangelical Council for Financial Accountability (ECFA) and an annual financial report is readily available for anyone requesting a copy.

For more information about World Help and our outreaches and programs, and to learn how you can join us in carrying out the Great Commission and the Great Commandment, visit our website at www.worldhelp.net.

They sleep on the streets.

They are cold and hungry.

They are frightened and alone.

THEY ARE FORGOTTEN!

The children of Northern Uganda have been slaughtered, raped, abducted, orphaned and terrorized. And still the horror continues. We must do something! Learn how you can save the life of a child who has been living a violent nightmare in Northern Uganda.

Find out more about these young victims of civil war by requesting your **FREE DVD** — *"Into Africa . . . The Compelling Story of the Forgotten Children"* — at **www.theforgottenchildren.com** or by calling **1-800-541-6691**.

If you can only do one thing in your lifetime,
let it be that you save the life of a child!

DOWNLOAD A FREE COPY RIGHT NOW!
www.worldhelp.net/forgottenchildren

Bring the mission field to your church.

World Help is proud to introduce the *Children of the World* International Children's Choir. Each year, a group of very special children, from many different countries, travels across the United States in an effort to raise awareness of the plight of homeless and orphaned children all over the world.

They will inspire you to change the world ... one child at a time.

If you are interested in scheduling *Children of the World* at your church, conference, school or special event, call toll free at 1-800-541-6691.

When you buy quality music CDs of Children of the World from our World Help online store, you help support our humanitarian and evangelistic work worldwide.

She has no one to count on but you.

Millions of children around the world suffer hardship, hunger and disease. They endure unimaginable living conditions without hope for a better future. Most will never be told that Jesus loves and cares for them.

God can use you to make a difference.

As a World Help child sponsor, you can ignite a spark of hope in the life of a child. You can become a special friend to a child who desperately needs someone to care.

Just $24 a month provides the basic necessities a child needs. Along with food, clothing, educational opportunities and medical attention comes the message that God loves them, and that a very special friend loves them too.

If you would like to sponsor a child, we will send you a packet containing your child's photograph and personal description. We will also show you how to develop a special relationship with your child by corresponding one-on-one with them. You will stay informed of your child's progress through periodic updates.

Make an eternal difference in the life of a child by becoming a child sponsor!

For more information, call 1-800-541-6691 or log onto our website at www.worldhelp.net.

Somewhere in the world a child awaits your compassionate response.
Please say "yes" today and give help and hope to a needy child.

STAY INFORMED!

Keep updated on all that you are accomplishing around the world through the many outreaches of World Help ...

... by logging onto www.worldhelp.net!

Our high-impact website will inform and inspire you! Take a look for yourself and you will be amazed at the colorful presentations ... the heart-touching stories and testimonies ... the incredible photography ... and the exciting on-line videos. This user-friendly site will take you through the many ministries and outreaches of World Help, as we share our vision and background, and let you know of opportunities that will allow you to step into the mission field from your own home. Check us out!

... by signing up for regular email reports!

Sign up today to receive regular updates and information about the outreaches and ministry opportunities of World Help via email. It's so quick and easy ... just go online at www.worldhelp.net and click on the "World Help Emails" icon. You will receive regular reports on the impact we are making around the world together in Christ's name.

Get your FREE
HOPE MAGAZINE
subscription!

This quarterly magazine will keep you updated on all our global work together. You will see vivid, 4-color photos of the very people you are impacting and read incredible testimonies of how God is using World Help through the prayers and support of friends like you.

This quality news publication will also address the latest issues, reports and needs from around the world and show how World Help is involved.

To view the latest issues of HOPE Magazine or sign up for your FREE subscription, go to www.worldhelp.net and click on "HOPE Magazine" under the "Get Involved" listing.

notes

NOTES

NOTES

NOTES

notes

NOTES